Stilled Tongues

Stephen Coleman

Stilled Tongues

From Soapbox to Soundbite

Porcupine Press

Porcupine Press, 10 Woburn Walk, London WC1H 0JL
© 1997 Porcupine Press
Interior layout and text processing by Paul Flewers
Cover design by Russell Herron
Printed in Britain by TJ Press
ISBN 1 89 943824 6

Contents

Preface

'BY "the public sphere" we mean first of all a realm of our social life in which something approaching public opinion can be formed. Access is guaranteed to all citizens. A portion of the public sphere comes into being in every conversation in which private individuals assemble to form a public body... Citizens behave as a public body when they confer in an unrestricted fashion — that is, with the guarantee of assembly and association and the freedom to express and publish their opinions — about matters of general interest. In a large public body this kind of communication requires specific means for transmitting information and influencing those who receive it.' (Jürgen Habermas, 'The Public Sphere: An Encyclopaedia Article', *New German Critique*, Autumn 1974)

'During the last 20 years there has been a revolution in the means of propaganda. The soap-box versus the wireless, the film and batteries of high-powered loudspeakers is as farcical as the bayonet versus the tank.' (Walter Padley, *Left*, no 99, January 1945)

'Since communication is the record of human growth, it has to be varied. It has to disperse itself into many different and independent systems... It has to get rid of the idea that communication is the business of a minority talking to, instructing, leading on, the majority. It has, finally, to get rid of the false ideology of communications as we have received it: the ideology of people who are interested in communications only as a way of controlling people, or of making money out of them.' (Raymond Williams, 'Communications and Community' in *Resources of Hope*)

'In its present form, equipment like television or film does not serve communication but prevents it. It allows no reciprocal action between transmitter and receiver; technically speaking, it reduces feedback to the lowest point compatible with the system.' (Hans Magnus Enzensberger, *The Consciousness Industry*)

'The radio would be the finest possible communication apparatus in public life, a vast network of pipes. That is to say, it would be if it knew how to receive as well as transmit, how to let the listener speak as well as hear, how to bring him into a relationship instead of isolating him. On this principle the radio should step out of the supply business and organise its listeners as suppliers.' (Bertolt Brecht, *The Radio as an Apparatus of Communication*)

'Without deliberation, democratic choices are not exercised in a meaningful way. If the preferences that determine the results of democratic procedures are unreflective or ignorant they lose their claim to political authority over us. Deliberation is necessary if the claims of democracy are not to be delegitimated.' (James S Fishkin, *Democracy and Deliberation*)

> Why don't our distinguished orators come forward as usual to make their speeches, say what they have to say?
> Because the barbarians are coming today and they're bored by rhetoric and public speaking.
> Why this sudden restlessness, this confusion?
> (How serious people's faces have become.)
> Why are the streets and squares emptying so rapidly, everyone going home so lost in thought?
> Because night has fallen and the barbarians have not come. And some who have just returned from the border say there are no barbarians any longer. (CP Cavafy, extract from *Waiting For The Barbarians*)

In the eighteenth century there existed a constitutional fiction which was used to justify the exclusion of the majority of the people from the franchise. It was known as virtual representation. The notion of the virtual vote was a deceit. In reality, a very small minority who owned most of the wealth decided who would be elected. Those without property qualifications permitting them to vote were outside the sphere of meaningful constitutional power. To be included virtually was in fact to be included not at all.

The fiction of virtual voting has now given place to a transformed notion of virtuality. Instead of virtual representation, late twentieth-century Britain is pervaded by the politics of virtual presentation. The essence of this new form of exclusion of the majority from the sphere of meaningful public discourse is to present constitutional democracy as if it is a spectacle to be produced by experts and observed by onlookers. Just as the eighteenth-century propertyless worker was deemed to be best served by the enfranchisement of his superiors on his behalf, so contemporary subject-cum-citizens rarely find themselves included directly in political debate. Public discussion has come to be regarded as a process in which an elite of respected political leaders, salaried commentators, both journalistic and academic, and public relations experts deliberate in virtue of the spectating majority. Kroker refers to this 'new global technological elite' as a 'virtual class'.[1]

The concept of public opinion, which once alluded to an inclusive, democratic public and the complexities of its autonomous deliberation, has evolved into a study of the scientific measurement of largely received views and their predictive value. As Merton and others have argued, focus group polling is different in that it explores how opinions are formed and changed.[2] But still the purpose of such methods of studying opinions is overwhelmingly concerned with the effects of presentation and predictive indications as to how existing policies can be presented better or other policies emphasised in order to contrive a situation more conducive to persuasive presentation. Focus group polling, far from empowering the 'ordinary people' whom it uses, is primarily a means of strengthening the grip of the presenters upon the minds of the receivers. There is nothing sinister or conspiratorial about this. Once political democracy is conceived largely as a spectacle, it is perfectly sensible that political communication should be conceived in terms of audience satisfaction rather than principled public deliberation.

A common defence of virtual presentation is that most people are not interested in political discussion, and are best served by a paternalistic communications system, and most accurately reflected intellectually by simple, snapshot polls. It is clearly correct to say that vast numbers of people are indifferent to much which passes for political debate. But this is a circular argument, for what passes as political debate usually fails to interact with the majority. Communication is seen as a process of a minority informing the majority. In such circumstances any degree of substantial interest from the public rather than mass disaffection should be a cause of surprise. What cannot be sustained is the contention that there is some kind of inherent antipathy on the part of the majority towards meaningful discussion. This is a claim shared by certain strands of conservative elitism and other strands of Leninist vanguardism, and both are wrong. To show how they are wrong requires the invocation of history. That is the main purpose of this book.

1. A Kroker, *The Possessed Individual: Technology and Postmodernity*, London, 1992.
2. RK Merton, 'The Focused Interview and Focus Groups: Continuities and Discontinuities, *Public Opinion Quarterly*, no 51, pp550-6.

I started to write this book with the conviction that humans are inherently and uniquely deliberative animals. The history of ideas, beyond the justifiably great works of the recognised canon, includes countless unrecorded, uncommented upon, ridiculed or patronised efforts by people to talk to one another about matters of more than mundane interest. Whether these were non-members of the priesthood daring to debate questions of theology, disenfranchised workers seeking the right to vote, or people on platforms in parks or on street corners arguing for their particular view of the world to be accepted, uncontrolled, unmediated and often unofficial discussion has gone on. This book is by no means an inclusive history of such discussion. It is confined to one country: Britain. Its examples are intended to be illustrative rather than encyclopaedic; whole areas of public discussion, both geographical and intellectual, are missing from this book. It is biased towards the study of open-air meetings rather than similar ones held in small halls, above pubs or in people's homes, largely because there is a vivid imagery of openness and expansive discussion in such settings. If I were reviewing this book as a critic, I would say that it errs on the side of a romantic depiction of its subject. My pre-emptive defence is to plead that there is nothing wrong in writing lovingly of sometimes unlovable people or events, as historians of parliament so often do, as long as such attachment does not impede the proper empirical search for evidence and commitment to candid interpretation.

Many scholarly volumes have been written about the theoretical justifications for and limitations of freedom of speech. These have ranged from erudite and valuable attempts to define the concept, to some rather superficial and academically parochial contributions relating to 'political correctness'. The problem with some of this political philosophy is the danger of it becoming lost in an ocean of abstraction. Without historical contextualisation, 'free speech', like so many other political concepts, can become rather amorphous. I assume in this book that it is better to let people say what they have to say than to stop them, and that a history of those with an interest in preventing people from having their way suggests a tension between two ideas of free speech. Ultimately, I am more interested in people speaking freely than people writing about whether or not they should be allowed to do so. Democracy without deliberation is a virtual sham, and recent attempts by democratic theorists to defend the deliberative scope of public action against the claims of 'postmodern' complexity and consequent bureaucratic elitism are much to be commended.[3]

3. See J Bohman, *Public Deliberation: Pluralism, Complexity and Democracy*, London,

I am painfully aware that I am probably of the last generation to have experienced the unique vivacity of the outdoor platform. Friends of the same age in the United States are too young to remember outdoor meetings, for they died out there and in other countries earlier than in Britain. I myself am too young to remember the days when the open-air platform was a feature of every district; a major means of political communication; something which was not a political eccentricity. My father, to whom I will always owe so much, was rarely happier than when soaking in the atmosphere of a public meeting. He never took the platform, but did not miss a chance to ask a pertinent question, to engage in the little group discussions around and after meetings, and to allow himself to become democratically immersed in the culture of open-minded discourse. I have sat since boyhood in election meetings of all parties, in the days when such direct appeals mattered, and delighted in the verbal exchanges amongst speakers, hecklers and questioners. I have attended open-air meetings from Speakers' Corner in London to Exchange Square in Glasgow. I have listened to and argued with nutcases, a few of whom I have seen in later years in positions of power. I have learned much about the art of democratic communication, often from speakers whose only social recognition has been on the platform.[4]

Much of the material in this book originated anecdotally from discussions with people who have been participants in democratic discussions of many kinds. In particular, I am indebted to Lord Soper, Tony Turner (who died while this book was being written) and Bobby Russell. Ron Cook was kind enough to send me much interesting material relating to Birmingham. Nicholas Salmon's doctoral research on William Morris has

---

1996; D Yankelovich, *Coming to Public Judgement: Making Democracy Work in a Complex World*, New York, 1991; and D Zolo, *Democracy and Complexity: A Realist Approach*, Cambridge, 1992.

4.   Nobody could accuse Tony Blair of any nostalgic yearnings for a return to the robust interaction of debate which once characterised the movement he is so eager to leave behind him. Leo Abse, in a scurrilous, mean-spirited but nonetheless often profoundly perceptive account of the Blair phenomenon, *The Man Behind the Smile* (London, 1996), cites Nye Bevan's view of those political actors whose speeches were 'fundamentally mimes subordinated to their parts in a performance'. 'As performing actors', comments Abse, 'they require decor, stage lighting, cosmetic treatments, designer advice, Sheffield razzmatazz. Those of us belonging to Old Labour took our agitations to the streets, spoke on our soapboxes and makeshift podiums in the parks, plinths and ramshackle halls of our towns, with no props, no amplifiers; we depended on our passions, our language and our authenticity to establish a rapport with those we sought to convince.' (p35)

helped me to write with accuracy about the free speech battles of the 1880s. I am grateful to Philip Wolmuth for the generous contribution of his photographs, some of which appear in this book. Many other people, too numerous to name, have passed me books, referred me to useful leads and offered their own recollections and insights. Whatever defects are to be found in this book, they are my responsibility, not theirs. Similarly, this book has drawn on many intellectual influences, as many as possible of which are cited. In particular, I owe much to reading Habermas for providing a framework for my thinking about the public sphere of discussion. Each time I turn again to the writings of Raymond Williams, my commitment to the real meaning of democratic communication is renewed, and I can only hope that this is reflected in my writing. I am grateful to Porcupine Press for having the confidence to publish this book, and in particular to Paul Flewers for efforts well beyond the call of duty and to Martin Jenkins for his ceaseless enthusiasm. Bernadette Coleman is to be thanked for allowing me the time and space to dedicate myself to this project while we were jointly engaged in the joyful ordeal of organising our wedding.

If this book is dedicated to anybody it is not to those mentioned in the pages which follow, but to those still languishing in prison cells, often faced with public neglect and institutionalised torture, simply for the crime of refusing to remain silent. May their voices be heard, and ours not drowned out.

Stephen Coleman
London
January 1997

Fools, Preachers and Troublemakers: The Silencing of the Common People

ON 16 December 1656 the British House of Commons resolved to bore a hole through the tongue of one James Nayler. This legalised barbarity was not a sadistic aberration; it was the outcome of six weeks of parliamentary debate concerning Nayler and the misuse of his tongue to speak freely.

Nayler was an active Quaker preacher who had written pamphlets and addressed crowds of people in the open air. In 1653 he had said of the interests represented by Church and government: 'God is against you covetous cruel oppressors who grind the faces of the poor and needy.' A year later, in the spirit of the Levellers, and even of Winstanley the Digger, he proclaimed that God 'made all men of one mould and one blood to dwell on the face of the earth'.[1] In 1656 Nayler's entry into the city of Bristol, where he had come to preach, was somewhat eccentric. Believing he was Christ, he rode on a donkey, and, ahead of him, a group of women strew palm leaves. The Christ-like imagery secured his arrest. The debate on his punishment commenced.

It was not just Nayler whom parliament wanted to teach a lesson. The early Quakers, with their passion for egalitarian, open preaching, often conducted with audiences of thousands upon the moors of northern England, were becoming a nuisance to authority. Their intellectual leader, Edward Burrough, conceded that the Quaker preacher was perceived to be 'a sower of sedition, or a subverter of the laws, *a turner of the world upside down*, a pestilent fellow'.[2] An enemy described them, with an ominous prescience of Nayler's fate, as 'men of acute wit and voluble tongues'. There was a solution for that.

When the matter came to parliament there was a good deal of anger

1. Cited in C Hill, *The World Turned Upside Down*, Harmondsworth, 1976, pp244, 248.
2. Cited in ibid, p245, my emphasis.

vented against these agitational orators. 'It has been always my opinion', declared Major-General Skippon, 'that the growth of these things is more dangerous than the most intestine or foreign enemies. I have often been troubled in my thoughts to think of this toleration... Their great growth and increase is too notorious, both in England and Ireland; their principles strike both at ministry and magistracy.'

The first inclination of parliament was to execute Nayler. A resolution to put this to the House was lost by 14 votes. There then followed the debate on 'the lesser punishment', as recorded by Thomas Burton in his *Parliamentary Diary*.

'Colonel White proposed that his tongue might be bore through.

'Colonel Barclay, that his hair might be cut off.

'Major-General Haines, that his tongue might be slit or bored through, and that he might be stigmatised with the letter B.'

A debate ensued. One Member argued that Nayler's hair should not be cut off in case this encourages a fashion for short hair; another that slitting his tongue would amount to punishment of death; Mr Downing asserted: 'You ought to do something with that tongue that has bored through God.' Some doubt existed as to the precise legality of excising a man's tongue. Major Audley informed the House: 'It is an ordinary punishment for swearing, I have known 20 bored through the tongue.' That seemed to settle it:

'Resolved, that his tongue be bored through.

'Resolved, that he be marked with the letter B in the forehead.

'Major-General Whalley proposed, that his lips might be slitted.

'Alderman Foot, that his head may be in the pillory, and that he be whipped from Westminster to the Old Exchange...

'Colonel Cromwell, that he may be whipped through the whole City from Westminster to Aldgate.'

There then followed much debate as to whether the punishment should be inflicted in London, Bristol, or some other place. The end result seems to have been that Nayler was whipped and bored through the tongue with a hot iron before more than one audience. Major-General Whalley told the House on 18 December of his pleasure at the punishment, for it would serve to warn others: 'Let them that commit James Nayler's fault, have his punishment.' And what precisely was his 'fault'? Mr Briscoe explained to the House: 'They meet in multitudes, and upon moors, in *terrorem populi*. I have a long time feared, that they and the people of a contrary judgement, should fall by the ears together.'

So, Nayler's penalty was to lose the use of his tongue. In other places and at other times, those guilty of listening to free speech have been parted from their ears.

The grotesque response by the state to the pursuit of free speech by James Nayler points to a profound paradox — a paradox which defines the historical tension explored in this study. Humans are animals with a unique nature. We are social to a degree of interdependent sophistication unknown within any other species. The most potent manifestation of such social sophistication is the capacity to communicate by the use of language. The degree to which other species can communicate meaningfully amongst themselves and with us is still a matter for scientific speculation and largely inconclusive research. There is no doubt about the fact that, whatever the ability of birds to communicate about migration, or squirrels to pass on knowledge regarding the location of nuts, humans are alone in being able to fashion speech in such a way as to influence the decisions of others within the species. The ancients' concern with rhetoric and the power of oratory was not a mere classical obsession concerning form, nor a subject pertaining to the particular political arrangements of the participatory politics of antiquity, but was a reflection of their understanding of this unique characteristic of humankind. We can speak. We can talk about mundane issues, but we can also become speakers: people seeking to use speech to influence the thought of others. In a highly literate culture (and also in a 'post-literate' society where communication is technologically mediated to a frightening extent), there is a tendency to diminish the significance of speech, speeches, speakers and the historical impact of words as weapons. It is important to remember that verbalised thought is a key defining quality of human biology and culture. Historically, this has not been forgotten by people enjoying powers which they have not wanted others to share or take away from them. An enormous amount of human energy has been utilised for the purpose of limiting or prohibiting the freedom to speak. This is the paradox: speech is our humanising power, but the power to dehumanise us by making us speechless has run through our history. The state's decision to remove radically the freedom of James Nayler to use his tongue and lips is but one graphic illustration of this paradoxical history.

Those who spoke out against medieval authority, mainly that of the unelected feudal state and the morally all-reaching Church, were deemed to be either fools or heretics. Heresy is the earliest symbol for intolerable speech, and, as we shall see, the first anti-speech laws and prosecutions fell under this rubric. But within the half-forgotten world of medieval verbal dissent there was one other strategy, the history of which is somewhat hazy and usually ignored: the freedom to resort to folly.

In one sense, the right to speak freely as a fool is both a perennial liberty and a response. To say what is forbidden is the universal prerogative of the jester, the half-wit and the crazed prophet. To dismiss as mere fools those who use their freedom to speak their minds, even where it does exist, as in the case of Speakers' Corner or the modern radio call-in programme, is an easy substitute for rationally confronting the substance of their comments. So, the fool has tended to be safe, if usually insignificant.

Who were the popular Fools of the Middle Ages, and what part did they play in permitting free comment to take place? On one level, these fools were wandering entertainers, entitled in the name of playfulness to satirise the authorities. Many of them would be wandering scholars (*vagi scolares*) or goliards. They would travel through towns and villages making witty observations about ecclesiastical and secular orthodoxy. Their public 'performances' (though the term is too formal) were a mixture of popular comedy and populist protest. They had a motive for their critical endeavours. The medieval monasteries suffered from a shortage of benefices in relation to the number of clergy within them. For some of the lesser clerics there was no other path to economic survival than to head for the road and collect money or alms in return for songs and wit. That their wit should have been sharpened in criticising the hypocrisy or mendacity of the Church was hardly surprising given that it was the insecurity of the overcrowded ecclesiastical sector which had forced them into vagabondage. As early as the twelfth century the Council of Rouen legislated against the right of clerics to be *vagi scolare*, and this was endorsed by subsequent Church Councils with increasing severity.[3] Not only did the monasteries provide the personnel for the Fools of the Middle Ages, but the universities did as well; many scholars simply lacked the means to support their studies, and therefore travelled the roads entertaining the peasants with speeches, mock disputations, and what would now be called nonsense poetry. Such Fools even claimed to belong to their own association, the *Ordo Vagorum*, but the evidence is that this was a mythical organisation. The Fools were a disparate crowd, playing mainly to the prejudices of their audiences, and propounding a kind of incoherent nihilism in response to the injustice of the world.

3. See Anton C Zijderveld, *Reality in a Looking-Glass: Rationality Through an Analysis of Traditional Folly* (London, 1982), especially Chapter 2, for an excellent account of the church's response to wandering scholars and Fools. See also Enid Welsford, *The Fool: His Social and Literary History* (Gloucester, Mass, 1966).

4

The Fools most certainly found audiences. The rarity of outspokenness within the confines of feudal ecclesiastical totalitarianism made Fools an obvious magnet for common folk enduring silent grievances. Equally rare was the opportunity for peasants to encounter intellectuals, albeit a foolish, counter-intelligentsia. The influence of the Fools' words was reflected in the frequent Church and state efforts to undermine their status and to stigmatise them. The final solution adopted, more or less simultaneously with the rise of capitalism, was for the Fool to be adopted by the state culture. By the sixteenth century the Fool had become a court employee, or a safely utilised theatrical wit. The Fool as vagabond, playfully cultivating free speech, was to become an anachronism, the final remnants of which were to be persecuted as pioneers of the 'mentally ill'.

The formulation of legal repression of free speech began with heresy. To oppose official Church dogma by words or deeds invited severe sanctions. The earliest recorded English case of such punitive action was in the mid-1160s, when some German-speaking *Publicani* were sentenced by an ecclesiastical court in Oxford to be branded and flogged. In 1210 an Albigensian heretic was burned in public in London. The most significant legal move against heretics came in 1400, when parliament, led by the Lords Temporal, passed the Statute of Heretics. This was designed primarily to suppress the Lollard agitation. On 2 March 1400 William Sawtre was put to the stake for speaking in opposition to the doctrine of transubstantiation. In fact, so eager were the Church authorities to make an example of Sawtre that he was burned before parliament had even finished enacting the Statute of Heretics. Fourteen years later the Statute was extended in a quite draconian fashion, and it was not repealed until 1677.[4]

An essential feature of free speech is the process of interaction between the speaker and the listener. Without the freedom to dissent verbally, and even to heckle, there is little point in listeners celebrating the freedom of the speaker. Churches have tended not to promote such interaction; the silence of the congregants, not coincidentally depicted as a flock, is a ritual requirement. Part of the emergence of free speech has been the listeners' insistence upon the freedom to become speakers.

An interesting case of this occurred in the reign of Mary Tudor. It had been the practice for some decades for Sunday sermons to be given outdoors at Paul's Cross in London. This open-air religious gathering allowed the Church to impart its message to its flock. The first such open-

---

4. See Hypatia Bradlaugh Bonner, *Penalties Upon Opinion*, London, 1934.

air sermon given during the reign of Mary resulted in heckling from the crowd, which grew so bad that the preacher, Gilbert Bourne, was nearly struck by a dagger thrown at him in the course of his sermon. The practice of open-air sermons was used less often after this occasion.[5] That this was not unprecedented is indicated by a statute passed in the reign of Edward VI which made it illegal to interrupt a minister in the course of the service. The full extent of heckling during Reformation church services is unrecorded, and will never be known.

It was in the 'revolutionary' years of the mid-seventeenth century that the interruption of sermons became a widespread practice. We are informed by Christopher Hill, in *The World Turned Upside Down*, that the Ranters were accused of interrupting church services, and one Hanserd Knollys created 'several riots and tumults' by visiting different churches, and speaking in response to the sermon. 'One can imagine the irritation this practice might cause', writes Hill, 'when, as time went on, the parson himself became the main target of itinerant interrupters, professionally skilled hecklers, denouncing his self-righteousness and his greed in taking tithes.' Indeed, the radical view came to be increasingly at odds with the very practice of paid preaching. Why should not the preachers speak both freely and for free? Payment for preaching was condemned by such radicals as the Digger preacher, Gerrard Winstanley, and William Walwyn, the Leveller, who suggested that the paid clergy 'pray, preach, and do all for money'.

The radicals of the English revolution tended to abandon the churches, and make for the streets. The activities of the 'mechanic preachers', who were lay clergy and artisan orators, are a key part of the founding of the outdoor speaking tradition in Britain. Their meetings invited questions and discussion, and their oratory owed as much to populism as to theology. They were an odd bunch of religious sects and individual philosophers: the Quakers, the Ranters, the Seekers, the Muggletonians, the Fifth Monarchists. The last were described by an opponent as 'the worst of men, the Scum and very froth of baseness', and even by one of their own preachers, Feake, as 'a company of illiterate men, and silly women'. In short, they were not of the establishment, and were self-educated.

Gerrard Winstanley first encountered Will Everard when the latter was preaching in the open outside the White Lion pub in Cobham. Everard was later to be arrested and thrown into jail for preaching in Kingston Market against the sin of private property.

5.   R Tittler, *The Reign of Mary I*, London, 1983, p46.

Of all the seventeenth-century people's orators — or 'mechanic preachers', as they were known — the most famous and probably the most influential was John Bunyan. Whilst stationed at Newport Pagnell in Buckinghamshire in the summer of 1645, as a member of the New Model Army, Bunyan might well have heard the preaching of Paul Hobson, one of the finest open-air preachers of his day. The atmosphere of widespread discussion within the army, combined with the growth of 'mechanic preachers' characterised by a marked contempt for the abstruse scholasticism of university-trained clerics, led Bunyan, once he had undergone the profound religious conversion so movingly described in his *Grace Abounding*, to become an itinerant preacher. In February 1658 he was first arrested for preaching, but it was his subsequent arrest in November 1660, under the Act of 1593 forbidding 'unlawful meetings and conventicles... calling together the people', that Bunyan was tried and convicted. He was to spend 12 years in prison for the crime of preaching without the state's permission, and for refusing to state that he would not do so in future.

The sneering derision with which mechanic preachers like Bunyan were treated by the authorities was well exemplified by Professor Thomas Smith, an Oxford scholar of Arabic, who heard Bunyan preach in Cambridgeshire, denied his right to do so, but refused to debate the matter with Bunyan on the grounds that the latter was a mere tinker whose capacity to pursue formal syllogistic discourse was manifestly lacking. Numerous were the disgusted accounts penned by established churchmen noting the popularity of the new preachers: 'Hardly one... had been a Fellow of a College, or had been at any time in the university; but poor scholars, servitors, and curates', wrote John Walker.[6]

George Fox, the founder of the Quakers, was fond of heckling official church sermons. It was as an open-air preacher that he excelled, and his writings are full of such accounts as the following: 'When I came from Whitehall to the Mermaid at Charing Cross, I stayed not long there, but went into the city of London, where we had great and powerful meetings. So great were the throngs of people that I could hardly get to and from the meetings for the crowds.' Like Bunyan, Fox spent time in prison for his dissenting activities.[7]

Many of the 'mechanic preachers' met to discuss their ideas in pubs. This was probably the beginning of that long radical tradition, as important as street meetings, of lofty discussion taking place within an atmos-

6. C Hill, *A Turbulent, Seditious and Factious People: John Bunyan and his Church, 1628-1688*, Oxford, 1988.
7. J Fryer (ed), *George Fox and the Children of the Light*, London, 1991, p89.

phere of beer and tobacco. Writing of the popular literary tradition of the mid-seventeenth century, Christopher Hill pointed out: 'Interregnum broadsides and pamphlets were read aloud to illiterate audiences in the alehouses and in the army.' The Levellers were the first British political organisation to conduct many of their meetings in pub rooms. Leveller activity laid the groundwork for future open-air propagandism. The gathering together of huge assemblies of people to support their petitions in 1647 and 1648 created London's first non-state-sponsored mass street meetings. Leveller speakers would address the crowds, and expect to have to answer questions and confront hecklers. Again, Leveller funerals were well-attended opportunities for the practice of radical oratory. The funeral of Robert Lockyer, a Leveller army mutineer who was shot, was an occasion for much street activity and much rhetoric from the platform.

Mid-seventeenth-century elections were again moments for unchecked street discussion to break out. In 1640 there was an increase in contested elections, and in boroughs such as Westminster, where there was a wider franchise than the national average, the tentative beginnings of open-air election meetings and popular street discussion emerged.

An important contribution to what might be described as the premodern tradition of public speaking was the Methodist tradition of field-preaching. In fact, John Wesley, the founder of Methodism, had initial doubts about this form of communication. When, on 2 April 1739, he acceded to George Whitefield's request to speak in the open air in Bristol, it was not without hesitation. He noted in his *Journal*:

'In the evening I reached Bristol, and met Mr Whitefield there. I could scarce reconcile myself at first to this strange way of preaching in the fields, of which he set me an example on Sunday; having been all my life (till very lately) so tenacious of every point relating to decency and order, that I should have thought the saving of souls almost a sin, if it had not been done in a church.'[8]

He was soon to become used to this method of preaching in the open, and, as Elisabeth Jay has observed in her introduction to selections from his *Journal*: 'Wesley developed a good eye for sites which offered good natural acoustics, shade from the sun, or shelter from the rain, but would preach above a hog-sty if it proved the only available venue.' So much of Wesley's preaching took place in the open air that Jay comments whimsi-

8. E Jay (ed), *The Journal of John Wesley: A Selection*, Oxford, 1987, p41.

cally: 'The *Journal* comes into its own as an account of climatic conditions in England between 1738 and 1790.'[9]

Considerable differences of style and motivation distinguished wandering Fools from field-preaching Methodists, but the connecting thread lay in a common regard for the public space as a free site for the unofficial communication of ideas for which no other forum existed.

The debate concerning the right to speak freely took political centre stage in the eighteenth century for the simple reason that it was then that an increasingly urbanised, politically disenfranchised population found a need to express itself. The state, confronted by that need, reacted in a number of ways, ranging from questioning the legality of open meetings, through passing repressive laws to make free speech illegal, to granting limited toleration to controlled dissent. The role of class in determining the state's response was paramount. In general, neither governments nor judges could see any harm in allowing men of substantial property to meet and discuss. These very few men were, after all, the electors of the government. Such men also had a right to petition the Crown with regard to the repeal of bad laws, or even the case for new laws based upon the improvement of their class interests. Since the parliaments of the last Tudor, and certainly after the constitutional upheavals of the Revolution, propertied voters had acquired a habit of discussing politics in a way that simply did not happen under the earlier Tudors. But these men, no less than the government, suffered deep political anxieties when it came to granting freedom of speech to two other classes: the disenfranchised gentry, including the new urban manufacturers and industrialists; and the increasingly articulate artisans. The history of the mid-eighteenth to mid-nineteenth centuries is in part a story of the alliance of these two excluded groups for political recognition and then, with the winning of respectability by the former, the unity of the former with the old aristocracy in repressing free speech for the working class.

The question of class not only determined who was thought fit to be allowed to speak, but how such speaking might be conducted. The brief and fragmentary history of free speakers that we have traced so far has emphasised the role of interaction, spontaneity of organisation, access to the platform for all, and the right to heckle as defining characteristics of the form of meetings, particularly those held in the open air where the control of landlords or even architectural constraints have been absent. Free speech required not only freedom from elitist exclusion by those

9.   Ibid, p xviii.

9

who thought that they had a right to monopolise discussion, but also freedom to pursue discussion outside of the convention-bound parameters of authoritarian, speaker-down debate. It was this democratic style of the growing movement for free speech, with its libertarian assumption that if speakers are higher than listeners it is only so that they can be heard, not because they are superior, which so scared the ruling elite. As it happens, much of this fear was unfounded. Much radical debate, whilst seeking to break the political monopoly of the elite, failed to go beyond the authoritarian boundaries of leaders and led. Whatever the undoubted dedication of men like Major Cartwright or Orator Hunt might have been, there is no sense in which such speakers could be described as 'one of the lads'.

It is sometimes suggested that free speech first became an issue in the course of the Wilkes Middlesex election campaign. This is not so. Prior to that there were several contested elections in which heated platform debates took place, and then in 1763 a hugely popular campaign led to several street meetings when the hapless government of Lord Bute proposed a bill in parliament to tax cider – and, furthermore, to search houses where it was suspected that cider was being made or stored. The *Annual Register* for 1763 records: 'The fury of the populace was let loose, and everything was full of tumult and disorder. Virulent libels, malicious beyond the example of former licentiousness, were circulated through the nation, in which nothing was sacred and no character was spared.' This was the year in which John Wilkes produced the infamous 'Number 45' of his scurrilous journal, *The North Briton*; an event which was to be of major importance in the history of the struggle for an uncensored press.

The case of Wilkes in the Middlesex election has been well documented.[10] In 1768 he was elected as Member of Parliament for Middlesex, only to be expelled in February 1769 for the 'crime' of having written a letter to the government which was regarded by the House of Commons as a 'seditious libel'. He was re-elected, but refused his seat by the Commons on the grounds that the election was void because parliament had expelled him. A month later Wilkes was elected again for Middlesex, was again refused his seat, and parliament then appointed as MP for Middlesex Colonel Luttrell, who had obtained less than a third of the votes won by Wilkes in the contest. The meetings to protest at this insolent governmental snub to the electors drew audiences of thousands, several of whom had no votes themselves. For most of these people the Wilkes

10. The best account is still IR Christie's *Wilkes and Liberty*.

campaign was their first exposure to the world of oratory. Those who had neither attended hustings for contested elections, nor been involved in the anti-Cider Tax campaign (which was largely confined to the cider-producing areas of western England), were discovering a new and intoxicating process whereby political ideas can be generated, influenced or destroyed by the power of the word. Great speakers like Major Cartwright and the fine rhetorician, Horne-Tooke, carved reputations for themselves in a hitherto little-known arena. The public outcry had its effect, and in the next general election, in 1774, Wilkes was elected once more for Middlesex, and was not prevented from taking his seat.

Ironically, the anti-Catholic Gordon Riots of 1780 were severely to damage the credibility of 'the common people' as responsible political participants, and one of the principal Members of Parliament physically and politically to aid the suppression of the riots and persecution of the rioters was John Wilkes.

The discrediting of outdoor agitation caused by the Gordon Riots was negligible compared to the stimulus to such activity generated by the French Revolution and the democratic phrases of Paine's *The Rights of Man*. The most tangible and enduring effect of this excitement was the formation in January 1792 of the London Corresponding Society. Although established by less than a dozen working men convening in a pub, within a short time the LCS had a membership of between 3000 and 5000. The important distinction of the LCS was that it was composed mainly of artisans. On 24 October 1793 the LCS held its first open-air meeting, in Hackney in East London. This drew a crowd of several hundreds. The second ever mass working class outdoor meeting was held at Primrose Hill on 14 April 1794.

Whilst these early meetings were taking place, state prosecutions were being organised. Reverend Winterbotham of Plymouth was indicted for using seditious words in his sermons in Plymouth; Thomas Briellat was found guilty of uttering seditious words whilst drinking in a public house; Dr William Hudson was convicted for using seditious language in a coffee house after having drunk two large glasses of punch. The men, whose trials were taken with astonishing seriousness by the state prosecutors, were sentenced to imprisonment of between one and two years each. More serious still was the trial of Thomas Muir in Edinburgh, who was accused of wickedly exciting people 'by means of seditious speeches and harangues' against the government. Government spies testified at the Muir trial, reporting the nature of his essentially democratic comments.

Of some legal importance in this trial was the prosecution assertion that the meetings addressed by Muir were unlawful because they were not summoned by legal authority. This relates to a commonly-held legal convention of the time, but not a law, that meetings could only be called lawfully by a Lord Lieutenant or County Sheriff. It was also held to be the case that only freeholders may legally attend such meetings. Muir was sentenced to transportation for a period of 14 years.

In 1795 the LCS was again running open-air meetings, this time in St George's Fields, Borough Road and Copenhagen Fields, Islington. Several thousands attended these meetings. There was more than one platform, which would have made it impossible for there to be any interactive relationship between speakers and audience: three platforms were put up, and people could wander from one to another, usually in pursuit of the more eloquent orators such as John Thelwall and John Gale Jones. But these meetings were held under a legal cloud, for in November 1795 the Pitt government passed the 'Two Acts' – the Treasonable Practices Act and, more relevantly, the Seditious Meetings Act 'for the more effectually preventing seditious meetings and assemblies'. The Bill, proposed by Lord Grenville, was intended to prevent gatherings of people for the purpose of petitioning parliament, and also to outlaw meetings held 'for the purpose of disseminating unjust grounds of jealousy, discontent, and false complaints... of irritating the minds of the people against their lawful governors...'. The act failed to stifle the LCS (in fact, its activities increased in the year after its passage), but this did not stop the intended atmosphere of intimidation and fear from prevailing.

In March 1796 the LCS sent John Gale Jones and John Binns to address a meeting in Birmingham, attempting to stay within the terms of the Seditious Meetings Act by ensuring that under 50 people would be present. Both men were arrested, and Gale Jones was convicted under the act. Three years later the government added to its statutes of repression the Corresponding Societies Act, which outlawed the LCS and other campaigns for constitutional reform. Together with a strengthened Seditious Meetings Act, whereby all meetings including historical lectures had to be licensed by a magistrate, and the suspension of *habeas corpus* (first suspended in May 1794), the state's repression of free speech was inclusive of most possible acts of public discussion.

As if the curtailment of free speech had not gone far enough by the turn of the century, the outbreak of the war against France legitimised even further repressive measures, and justified a feeling of suspicion directed towards those who favoured social or political change. They were depicted as the English Jacobins (a term in fact which some of them applied to themselves), and the link between the advocates of Reform and the French Terror was not dissimilar to that made between socialists who opposed early twentieth-century capitalism (including those who rejected Bolshevism) and the Red Terror of post-revolutionary Russia. In the first decade of the nineteenth century reformers were well advised to lie low — and most of them did.

After the war, in November 1816, an open-air meeting was held at Spa Fields in Manchester. It was addressed by Henry Hunt, a man regarded by Francis Place as 'the best mob orator of the day, if not, indeed, the best which had ever existed'. Known to the crowds as 'Orator Hunt', the star of the Spa Fields meeting was a politically moderate character with no revolutionary inclinations, and a preoccupation with his own enormous ego. Following the meetings at Spa Fields (there were two) some minor rioting and politically adventurist gestures were indulged in by a few agitated workers. These were a small minority of those present.

The government's response was to set up investigations into the dangers associated with the meetings and petitions which were abounding. The Lords Secret Committee reported that the radical societies were taking 'advantage of the opportunities afforded by public meetings', where they 'address the multitude in terms of unprecedented licence and violence, amounting even in some instances to an open declaration that, in case of non-compliance with their Petitions, the Sovereign will have forfeited his claims to their allegiance'.[11]

In 1817 parliament responded to its Secret Committees by passing four acts, the most far-reaching of which was a new Seditious Meetings Act introduced by Lord Castlereagh. He warned the House against the base passions of the 'mob', whom he called a 'deluded rabble', driven to 'the most horrid excesses and crimes' by the harangues of the public speakers. What were the terms of the Act? All meetings of more than 50 people held for the purpose of altering the affairs of church or state were unlawful unless a notice of intention to hold such a meeting was published in a newspaper and signed by seven householders five days before the meeting was to take place. Copies of the notice had to be sent to at least three local Justices. Magistrates were entitled to attend all such meetings, and to close them at will. If more than 12 people remained after the magistrate's order to disperse, this crime would be punishable by

11. Lords Secret Committee, *Parliamentary Debates*, Volume 35, p416.

death. The Act made it illegal to allow a field or other open space, as well as private rooms or halls, to be used for the purpose of holding a meeting unless a magistrate had granted a licence for meetings to take place. Any person attending corresponding clubs was liable to a penalty of seven years transportation if convicted on indictment.

The repressive legislation did not meet with total submission. On 10 March 1817 a crowd of several thousand workers assembled at St Peter's Field in Manchester. Their intention was to petition against the curtailment of free speech, especially the suspension of *habeas corpus*. Several of them planned to march to London, so many in the crowd carried blankets to sleep on during the journey; hence the usual reference to this meeting as the gathering of the Blanketeers. Within a short time a magistrate came to the meeting and read the 1715 Riot Act. The militia was used to disperse the crowd and there were 29 arrests. (A few of the Blanketeers embarked upon their march to London, but only half a dozen reached even as far as Ashbourne Bridge in Derbyshire.)

Other meetings did take place illegally: on Hunslet Moor near Leeds, where the unemployed gathered twice in June 1819; in Ashton-under-Lyne; on Newhall Hill, Birmingham in July. At the end of July the Prince Regent issued a proclamation calling upon the magistrates to bring to justice those 'who had been or may be guilty of uttering seditious speeches or harangues'. The wording of this advice was ominous: not only should those making so-called seditious speeches be arrested, but so should those who 'may be guilty'. The ground was being prepared for a major state assault against the public platform. But the immediate effect of the proclamation was one of impotence. At the end of July a large outdoor meeting in Huddersfield was addressed by two workers; a shoemaker and a weaver. (Thomas Hardy, the Secretary of the LCS, was a shoemaker.) There were further meetings in Birmingham, Leigh and Stockport.

On 16 August a huge meeting, to be addressed by Hunt, was planned for St Peter's Field in Manchester. The bloodstained events of that day, known as the Peterloo massacre, are well documented. On the order of the magistrates the cavalry, equipped with sabres, launched into the crowd of between 60 000 and 80 000 people. Samuel Bamford, who was present, records in his *Passages in the Life of a Radical*, how the meeting had been an orderly affair, when, thinking that they were hearing the approach of marchers from Blackburn to join the assembly, it transpired that the cavalry, with swords in hand, were trotting towards them:

14

'"The soldiers are here", I said, "we must go back and see what this means." "Oh", someone made reply, "they are only come to be ready if there should be any disturbance in the meeting." "Well, let us go back", I said, and we forced our way towards the colours. On the cavalry drawing up they were received with a shout, of good will, as I understood it. They shouted again, waving their sabres over their heads; and then, slackening rein, and striking spur into their steeds, they dashed forward, and began cutting the people.'[12]

This legitimised massacre lasted for less than quarter of an hour. After it, recorded Bamford:

'The hustings remained, with a few broken and hewed flag-staves erect, and a torn and gashed banner or two dropping; whilst over the whole field, were strewed caps, bonnets, hats, shawls and shoes, and other parts of male and female dress; trampled, torn and bloody. The yeomanry had dismounted — some were easing their horses' girths, others adjusting their accoutrements; and some were wiping their sabres. Several mounds of human beings still remained where they had fallen, crushed down, and smothered. Some of these still groaning — others with staring eyes, were gasping for breath, and others would never breathe more. All was silent save those low sounds, and the occasional snorting and pawing of steeds.'[13]

This was the desired result of Lord Liverpool's Tory government. 'All was silent' except for the horses whose voices contained no words, no danger. Eleven people were killed at Peterloo, and over 500 were wounded, about 140 by sabres.

The response of the government to Peterloo was to strengthen the repressive legislation. The infamous 'Six Acts' were passed, one of which was the Seditious Meetings and Assemblies Prevention Act. This was even more strict in its control over public meetings than the acts of 1795 and 1817. In future, magistrates not only required notification five days before any meeting was held, but were empowered to change the date, time or location of the meeting. Furthermore, the act made it illegal for non-local people to attend meetings in a particular area. A meeting planned for a particular parish, district, borough or county therefore could only

12. S Bamford, *Passages in the Life of a Radical*, original London, 1844, reprinted Oxford, 1984, p152.
13. Ibid, p153.

lawfully have in attendance people residing in the specified area. The freedom to choose which meeting to attend was thereby abolished. Those holding meetings in contravention of the act were liable to a penalty of seven years transportation. The new law was vigorously defended in both Houses of Parliament, by such men as Mr Plunket in the Commons, who stated: 'If bodies of the people not convened by any public functionary, but called together by mountebanks whose only title was their impudence and folly, were entitled to assemble in tens of thousands... there was an end to the Constitution.'

Lord Castlereagh, proposing the new law in the House of Lords, stated:

'Any assembly of the people, whether armed or unarmed, whether using or threatening to use force, *or not doing so*, and whether the avowed object was illegal or legal, if held in such numbers, or with such language or emblems, or deportment, as to create well-grounded terror in the King's liege subjects for their lives, their persons or their property, was an illegal assembly, and might be dispersed as such.'

In short, even if a meeting neither used nor threatened force, and was perfectly legal, if it led to fear in the minds of those concerned with their property – to take just one of the three fears – the lawful meeting could be declared illegal and broken up, as had been done in Manchester.

Ten of the leading activists at Peterloo were arrested and tried in March 1820. At first the government attempted to convict them for high treason, but this was so manifestly absurd that in the end they were convicted on the grounds that they 'unlawfully, maliciously and seditiously did meet and assemble themselves together, with diverse other persons, for the purpose of raising and exciting discontent and disaffection in the minds of the liege subjects of the King, and for the purpose of moving and exciting them to hatred and contempt of the Government...'. Hunt was sentenced to imprisonment for two-and-a-half years, and Bamford and two others were sent to prison for one year. Bamford's account of his imprisonment is in his memoirs.

In May 1821 an attempt was made in parliament to repeal the Seditious Meetings Act. In 1824, the year that parliament repealed its notorious laws banning trade union combination, the Seditious Meetings Act expired and was not renewed.

After 1825 the struggle for free speech changed significantly. With the coming to power of Grey's Whig government in 1830 came the recognition that the industrial middle class must be politically empowered; as capital became enfranchised, and new laws came to reflect a state understanding of the need for industrial regimentation, the fragile extra-parliamentary alliance between capitalists and workers collapsed. Increasingly the liberal — and Liberal — middle class came to fear the unchecked exercise of free speech by those who were, after all, their employees. Looked at on a broad canvas, the change is vivid. In the Wilkes campaign, urban manufacturers welcomed the support of their fellow voteless artisans in the streets; by the time of Peterloo the workers composed the majority in the agitation, but still there was solid radical Whig support for their rights — after all, Hunt was dedicating his rhetoric to the great liberal cause of Reform. The riots of 1831 were the last moment of cross-class unity: workers threw stones at the windows of aristocratic homes so that their employers could have the vote. After 1832, with not only the Reform Act, but the Factory Act and Poor Law Amendment Act, many workers saw little to hope for from the Whigs, but, more importantly, the newly-enfranchised began to experience the sense of danger and contempt long felt by the old aristocracy when they looked upon the vocal working class. Henry Jephson's great liberal study, *The Platform: Its Rise and Progress*,[14] is a perfect illustration of this process of redefinition of the value of free speech. The first volume is a splendid work of unashamed defence of the Englishman's right to take to the platform. (This study has drawn upon its detailed information.) In the second volume, commencing roughly at the time of the agitation for the Reform Bill, Jephson's impatience at the robust and sometimes crude oratory of the new proletarian platform speakers is undisguised. He has a scarcely concealed contempt for the inflammatory rhetoric of Chartism. *The History of the Chartist Movement*, written by his contemporary, Gammage, himself a Chartist orator, is referred to as 'rambling, ill-arranged and illiterate'.[15] When workers in the North went on strike in defence of the Charter, for Jephson 'the Platform had reached its lowest depths', and he quotes approvingly from a speech made by John Bright 'to the men of Rochdale':

'Your speakers talk loudly. They tell you of your numbers and your power, and they promise you marvellous results if you will but be firm. They deceive you; perhaps they are themselves deceived. Some of them contrive to live on this deception, and some are content with the glory of their leadership. They flatter you grossly, and they as grossly calumniate

14. H Jephson, *The Platform: Its Rise and Progress*, Volumes 1 and 2, London, 1892.
15. Ibid, Volume 2, p197.

your employers. They pretend to be working out your political freedom; they know that that freedom can only be obtained through the electoral body and the middle classes, and yet they incessantly abuse the parties whom it is your interest to conciliate and convince.'[16]

Bright's criticism says much in a short space about the liberal/Liberal disenchantment with the new uses of open-air meetings. 'Your speakers talk loudly'; this is both a rejection of form and content. In form, the thrown voices of the working class orators were an inevitable consequence of the physical environment in which they had to speak. Parliamentary debate can take place in the closed, sedate atmosphere of an acoustically well-designed chamber. Addresses at political banquets, which after the 1830s became a main form taken by the non-working class platform, are within an environment of relaxation and close proximity between speaker and addressed. The same congenial conditions apply to the university lecture or speech. But outdoor orators have never had such facilities. To be heard the less experienced must shout, and the skilled orators must still throw their voice. They must 'talk loudly', or they would be inconspicuous. But the accusation of loudness was probably not only a criticism of volume. A similar recognition of rhetorical loudness has been associated in the twentieth century with black civil rights orators in the United States; it is hardly surprising that people who are brought up to feel that nobody will listen to them, that they have no reason to expect to be heard, when they do speak out will likely do so either with the humble timidity of those expecting to be ignored, or with the loud voice of speakers who must literally compete for a hearing. This applied no less to working class Chartists than to radical black Americans, and as the stridency of the latter might offend the sensibilities of certain racists, so the loud oratory of the Chartist speakers was a source of complaint for Bright.

The complaint that the Chartists failed to use the platform to encourage workers to accept the leadership of their employers is the beginning of that response which has been at other times applied to trade unionism: combination is all very well, but would it not be better to combine under the guidance of those against whom you are resisting? As to the warning against being promised too much, this is but an early blow in the rhetoric of anti-socialist propaganda, to which James Connolly responded: 'We only want the Earth.'[17]

16. Ibid, pp197-8.
17. P Berresford Ellis (ed), *James Connolly: Selected Writings*, Harmondsworth, 1973, pp292-3.

It was as participants in the Chartist movement that workers came into their own as platform speakers. As Gammage, who was one of them, rightly observes, prior to Chartism 'even the more enlightened of the working class had been but little accustomed to public speaking. The platform had been almost exclusively occupied by the upper and middle classes, and it could hardly be expected that the working men, deprived in a great measure of educational advantages, would become adept speakers in a day.'[18]

It was in the embryonic period of Chartism, before the second Petition of 1842, that the most momentous occasions of open-air oratory were witnessed. In these early years speakers were acquiring the skills of moving audiences, and listeners were learning the importance of live democratic debate. After the second Chartist Petition, the movement became increasingly embroiled in internal feuding, the reputations of speakers became tarnished, the tactic of working class violence began to find sympathy amongst those frustrated at the slowness of street discussion and the state's repressive response to it. But the early months and years were a time of innocence when crowds would wrestle to be close to the scenes of the great orations of hope.

Huge meetings were held in Glasgow, Newcastle, Birmingham and Palace Yard, London in the spring and summer of 1838. At Glasgow Green, on 28 May, an audience numbering tens of thousands listened to Chartist orators brought up from Birmingham and London. On 27 June vast crowds from Newcastle gathered on the Town Moor, where rousing speeches were given and cheered. The audience comprised women as well as men. 'The women... vied with the men in their eagerness to listen to the fiery words of political inspiration', Gammage tells us. Indeed, many of these meetings were organised not only for discussion, but as spectacles of strength; banners, bands and symbolic emblems of freedom added to the sense of solidarity. Such features characterised the vastly attended meetings, but most meetings were not of this kind. In towns and villages across the country, newly-constructed platforms were erected, and frequently unchronicled speeches met with applause, cheers, laughter and much interruption for questions.

Within a short time there emerged a gallery of the most popular and effective orators. There is something of the free market about public speaking; no amount of publicity or self-conceit could make a speaker

18. RC Gammage, *History of the Chartist Movement, 1837-1854*, originally 1894, reprinted London, 1969, p17.

appealing to a bored crowd. The audience could vote with their feet, and an orator would have either to improve or give up. The speakers who knew how to 'work' an audience were in constant demand.

By most accounts, the greatest of the early Chartist orators was Henry Vincent, who had first ascended the outdoor platform in Hull at the age of 13. 'For fluency of speech he rivalled all his contemporaries, few of whom were anxious to stand beside him on the platform', wrote Gammage. Vincent seems to have possessed all of the abilities of the popular open-air speaker, the most important of which is probably the ability to make a crowd laugh. (Laughter is one of the few collective actions, apart from clapping or cheering – or, worse still, chanting – that a speaker can stimulate in an audience as a sign of their support.) Vincent was a good impressionist, had a musical voice, and possessed the rare ability, embarrassing when misapplied, to move from gravity to humour at will. The Chartist crowds regarded him as 'the young Demosthenes of English Democracy'. Strangely, Gammage, who shared the popular partiality for Vincent's oratory, regarded him as being an essentially superficial speaker. Yet is this so strange? Open-air meetings, particularly the vast ones at which Henry Vincent was so often used to rouse the crowd, are not occasions for sustained logical discourse. This is not to say that rational discussion could not prevail on such occasions; as we shall see, that was to be a view put forward by those who would ban them. But there must be a difference between an elaborated case presented in a lecture hall and a stirring platform oration, which need not be a harangue, but is almost bound to err on the side of generality, and to appeal to experience.

Vincent was not the only popular Chartist speaker. There was Feargus O'Connor, the ex-MP for Cork, who claimed to be descended from Irish kings; Robert Lowery, the Newcastle Chartist, regarded him as having 'a good voice, a ready Irish wit, and oratorical flourish. Being a barrister, he was an adept at special pleading, and had much tact to please those whom he wanted.' But, according to Lowery, whose assessment is not unrepresentative of his fellow Chartists, O'Connor was 'no reasoner', and 'his vanity and self-esteem were diseased, and upset all the rest of his powers'[19]. Of an equally fiery reputation was the Reverend Joseph Rayner Stephens, a speaker, who, according to Lowery, was most impressive at relating general principles to what he called 'knife and fork questions'. He had been dismissed as a Wesleyan preacher, and he became the most

19. B Harrison and P Hollis (eds), *Robert Lowery: Radical and Chartist*, London, 1979, p125.

popular of the Chartist orators in Lancashire. Bronterre O'Brien, who was better as a writer and indoor lecturer than on the outdoor platform, was christened by Feargus O'Connor 'the schoolmaster' of the movement. Gammage was greatly impressed by O'Brien, commenting: 'No other speaker was capable of rising to such a height, or of so impressing an audience with the strength and intensity of his feelings... No man could so easily mould reason, satire or declamation into one compact body, or hurl the triple weapon at the head of an antagonist with more terrible force.'[20] There were other great Chartist orators, many of whom were associated with their own localities: Augustus Beaumont, James Ayr and Robert Lowery in Newcastle; George Binns and James Williams in Sunderland; the Scot, Abraham Duncan. Many others carved out reputations in village squares and main streets of towns where their efforts became part of the local political culture. In the strike wave of 1842 such speaking experience was put to good use in explaining the cause of the strikes and raising the morale of the strikers.

In the autobiography of Robert Lowery, the Newcastle tailor who came to be one of the prominent speakers for the movement, we learn a great deal about how Chartist speakers were made. Lowery's formal education ended when he was nine, but at the age of 21 his political education was exposed to the 'philosophic astuteness, literary ability, [and] oratorical powers' of the speakers for the Northern Political Union who spoke in favour of the 1832 Reform Act. At about this time he helped to form a debating society comprising 'about 20 members of the mechanic and shopkeeping trades'. The society met weekly, and 'admitted the discussion of any subject but polemical divinity'. Before long Lowery was called upon to propose a toast in support of the Polish insurrection at a big meeting organised by the society. This filled him with trepidation, and he began to prepare himself for the challenge:

'I took a walk into the neighbouring fields in the afternoon until I got to an elevated part of one, where I could see all round, and thus know if any person was approaching within the sound of my voice. I tried to conceive the full town and manner of speech which I thought it necessary I should deliver, and see how long I could sustain myself without faltering for matter or expression. This I did, and I remember well there was a flock of sheep grazing close by, and they were on the whole perhaps a superior audience to many, for if they did not reflect on what I said, they were

20. Gammage, op cit, pp76-7.

quiet and orderly; they did not run away, but remained to the end, and there were some old ewes and rams, which occasionally turned up their countenances and observed me with serious gravity. I satisfied myself that I could "talk awhile".'

On 15 July Lowery addressed his first open-air meeting before an audience of some 10 000 people who attended what was originally planned as an indoor meeting protesting against the Irish Coercion Bill. This led to further outdoor speaking. The following April he addressed an audience of 100 000 gathered in the Town Moor to protest against the transportation of the Tolpuddle Martyrs.

Lowery supported the Charter, and became one of the best speakers in its defence. 'For solidity and clearness of argument he excelled the majority of speakers', observed Gammage. Lowery became a full-time speaker, employed by Robert Blakey, owner of the radical *Northern Liberator*, to travel around the Tyne and Wear region, addressing questions of the day, and promoting the circulation of the newspaper. In the next three years, before he left the Chartist movement and became a temperance advocate, Lowery travelled as far north as Scotland and south as Truro in Cornwall, speaking to working class audiences in the open air. Lowery never ceased to be impressed by the dignity and thoughtfulness of his audiences: 'I was astonished at the number of people who gathered at the meetings. The distance which many of them came, and their earnest attention, showed a great interest in the cause. I was also much delighted at the intelligence of those with whom I conversed.'

By the autumn of 1838 the ritual of holding 'torch-light meetings' commenced. These were meeting held at night, this being the most convenient time for most workers to attend on a regular basis. They were often preceded by a procession, and involved a good deal of symbolic imagery. These events clearly frightened many members of the middle class, and associations were formed to protect themselves and their property. A Proclamation from the government followed, declaring the torch-light meetings to be illegal. In part this was a response to the increasingly violent language of O'Connor and Stephens, and those who adhered to their 'physical force' strategy. Indeed, Stephens was arrested and charged with using seditious language from the platform. (At his trial he capitulated utterly, renounced physical force, and urged the working class to submit peacefully to their lot in life.) That the physical force faction played into the hands of the government by issuing threats of civil war which they could not have backed up is clear, but it is also evident that the government wanted to suppress the unchecked public discussion which was breaking out across the country.

On 5 July a peaceful gathering assembled for a Chartist meeting in the Bull Ring in Birmingham. Such meetings had been held there regularly. 'From January', writes George Barnsby in his history of Birmingham labour, 'the Birmingham working class had taken to meeting in the Bull Ring to discuss politics and to have read aloud... the working class newspapers of the week. These meetings began at 8pm and were at first attended by only 200 to 300 people.' By May the meetings were being held twice daily, and were attended by crowds of thousands who would assemble to hear the Chartist orators, most notably John Fussell. On 11 May the city authorities issued posters threatening to prosecute those attending meetings in the Bull Ring. Attempts to stop the meetings, including the arrest of Fussell by two police officers brought up from London, were unsuccessful. Between 5 and 15 July the Bull Ring meetings were invaded by a contingent of 60 police officers who had been brought by train from London for the purpose. They attacked the crowd, ordering them to disperse, and the mayor read the Riot Act. There had been no riot in the Bull Ring prior to the arrival of the metropolitan police. It was only after the attack that the crowd resisted, and several arrests were made. The Chartist Convention was meeting in Birmingham at the time, and the next evening, by which time martial law had been declared in the city and police and soldiers paraded through the streets, the Convention resolved 'that a wanton, flagrant and unjust outrage has been made upon the people of Birmingham, by a bloodthirsty and unconstitutional force from London... that the people of Birmingham are the best judges of their own right to meet in the Bull Ring or elsewhere...'. Lovett, who signed the statement on behalf of the Convention, and Collins, who published it, were then arrested and subsequently sentenced to 12 months imprisonment.[21] The Bull Ring repression commenced a year-long process of arrests, trials for sedition, and attempts to intimidate workers into public silence. The state's policy partly succeeded; in several areas meetings retreated from the streets into private rooms or lecture halls. The harshness of the state drove more workers into the physical force wing of the movement, and sorry episodes such as the hopeless insurrection of 1839 in Newport occurred, in part at least, because belief in victory by the moral force of open persuasion had been discredited.

21. GJ Barnsby, *Birmingham Working People: A History of the Labour Movement in Birmingham, 1650-1914*, Wolverhampton, 1989, pp82-6.

The harassment of meetings and the imprisonment of speakers and organisers forced Chartism towards a strategy which could only end in failure. Though fearful of the more outlandish Chartist threats in 1848, the rulers of Britain felt happier arming their state forces to confront an illusory revolutionary force on Kennington Common than they had done when hundreds of meetings in the first phase of Chartism had been challenging their right to a monopoly of power. The threatened violence of the working class can always be met by the superior weaponry of the state. It is the vociferous and articulate stirrings which have always posed the most dangerous threat. The ranks of the impoverished armed with sticks and pikes can always be defeated. But what do you do with tongues that persist in their subversive wagging?

From the Gallows to the Soapbox

HAVING commenced with a dramatic account of torturous excision, the early state's radical response to unwanted speech, we turn now to an even more final extremity of state repression. What was to be done with the insolent violators of the all-dominating property relationships? Between 1196 and 1783 approximately 50 000 of them were hanged in public. Their state-organised murder was to serve as a lesson to the unpropertied *mobile vulgus*: the frightened, enraptured audience at the macabre theatrical spectacle of vengeance and order.

Ironically, but almost certainly not coincidentally, it is on the very spot upon which so much blood had been legally spilt that the eccentric and historically dismissed institution of Speakers' Corner came to stand. On a sunny afternoon in the late twentieth century it is possible with no great strain of the historical imagination to hear the yells of hanging wretches and merrily gawping onlookers as distinct echoes in the air. For them the spectacle involved as its penultimate act the 'last dying speech' (as it was called from the sixteenth century onwards) of the condemned man or woman — indeed, there were women too: about the same ratio as those on the modern platforms at Speakers' Corner.

It is worth returning to that pre-incarnation of Speakers' Corner, for perhaps its ritualistic function will tell us something about the echo which we now hear.

Tyburn Tree was one of several points in London where public hangings were held, but over time it became the most attractive and notorious, drawing bigger audiences than its rival killing exhibitions, and leading to the places of execution as far away as Dublin, Liverpool and York being known as 'Tyburn'.[1] The name of the hanging tree was derived from what is now a subterranean brook beneath Brook Street: Tye Bourne. The tree stood at the junction of Tyburn Road (now Oxford Street) and Tyburn Lane (now Park Lane). Standing on the north-east corner of Hyde Park,

---

1. See Alfred Marks, *Tyburn Tree: Its History and Annals*, London, 1910.

the hanging tree dominated the popular geography of the area. The hanging structure itself was 12 feet in height, triangular in shape, and capable of hanging eight people on each of its three sides. (It was often said that the western side, facing Paddington, was reserved for Catholics.) Known colloquially as the Three-Legged Mare and the Three-Legged Stool, Tyburn Tree stood as a permanent warning to those who produced but did not possess. Well might the audience of Shakespeare's *Love's Labour's Lost* have shuddered at Berowne's reference to Tyburn, the scene of what *The Daily Graphic* was later to call 'probably the most blood-saturated spot in all London'.

Yet it was in connection with this spot that some of the most powerful rituals of public speaking and collective listening were to emerge. The role of the crowd began well before the hanging: at the trial of the accused, or rather as excluded onlookers at the court whose own judicial invisibility (as propertyless workers) forced them to invent their own counter-hearing: the popular, but impotent justice of the courtyard and the ale-house.[2] With reference to an account from 1732 of the scene outside the Old Bailey in 1715 when one Thomas Smout was being tried for his life after shouting in public, 'God damn King George', we hear of how the excluded crowd formed 'themselves into Committees of threes, fours and fives, all over the Session-house-yard, and there debate of the Fates and Circumstances of the Criminals, till the latest Hour of the Court's sitting'. Denied the freedom to comment openly upon the social business of life, it was in the prelude to the death of one of their own that working class discussion was tolerated, if not encouraged.

There were eight hanging days each year, and we know that these excited the greatest public interest. Partly drawn by bored or sadistic enchantment, and partly invited as guests to a moral exhibition for their own ideological welfare, there was another reason for the Tyburn turnout: here was an all too rare occasion for permissible public comment. Those who thought that hanging was too good for the condemned wretch were allowed to say so, and furthermore to make the pain and humiliation of the last moments a greater mental and physical torment than they would otherwise have been. Those who sympathised with the condemned were allowed to utter their sentiments, this pathos adding to the theatricality of the ritual. The condition of such freedom to speak was the un-

2. Peter Linebaugh's *The London Hanged: Crime and Civil Society in the Eighteenth Century* (London, 1991) provides a brilliant analysis of this aspect of public discussion and entertainment beyond the state judicial system.

derstanding that the crowd may regret but never doubt the verdict of guilt over which they could have no control.

So, when the romantic highwayman, Claude Duval, was hanged at Tyburn on 21 January 1670, the epitaph which followed him well reflected the mood of his female sympathisers in the crowd: 'Here lies Du Vall: reader, if male thou art, Look to thy purse; if female, to thy heart.'

On hanging days at Tyburn the crowds were frequently so great that tickets were sold for up to half a crown so that the more affluent onlookers could have decent seats. Most people stood. The ritual of the condemned procession need not detain us at length. The convicts to be hanged were conveyed to Tyburn from Newgate prison (the site of what is now the Old Bailey) in a cart. The City Marshal rode in front, and a company of redcoats at the rear. The procession stopped twice on its way, once at St Sepulchre's Church, where the condemned were given nosegays or sometimes oranges, and then at St Giles, where they were given beer: the last beverage they would taste. Perhaps this was to prepare them for the ritual of the 'last dying speech'. (A plaque outside The Masons Arms public house in Seymour Street declares that its cellar was used to house victims prior to their executions, and was connected to the site of the gallows by an underground passage. Perhaps here lies a clue to the alcoholic stimulus which led so many of the condemned to loquacious exhibitions in their final moments.)

The speeches of the condemned can be regarded as the first early examples of popular open-air free speeches in English history. But we should not greet such early free speech with too much enthusiasm. Firstly, it was hardly a product of liberty; on the contrary, its existence resulted from vicious legal repressiveness which made it possible only at the point of execution to speak one's mind in public. Secondly, the record of most 'last dying speeches' shows that they were far from being subversive, or even dissentient, moments of unchecked public speech. Most of the recorded speeches take the form of public confessions, not only for the crime committed, but for lives characterised by nothing less than the inheritance of Adamic sin. It was the job of the Ordinary of Newgate, who performed the role of a prison chaplain-cum-broadsheet publisher, to interview the condemned and write up their final speeches. *The Ordinary of Newgate, His Account of the Behaviour, Confession, and Dying Words of the Malefactors who were Executed at Tyburn* stands as the official record of these 'last dying speeches', and it was supplemented, for the benefit of wider public consumption, by broadsheets and cheap transcripts of the speeches, several of which were very popular indeed. Charles Hindley, the collector of *Curiosities of Street Literature*, in his second volume on the gallows literature of the streets, states that the broadsheets following the hangings of Manning and Reed reached record sales of two-and-a-half million copies.

The Ordinary, in his *Account*, interviewed the condemned on the wrongness of their crimes, and included, as well as their speeches, theological as well as legal explanations of their wrongdoing. The object was clearly propagandistic. Again, the condemned, in their final utterances from the cart beneath the gallows, must have been under a huge pressure to speak repentantly, firstly, because of the hope of a last-minute reprieve from the civil authorities (which did happen sometimes, much to the crowd's excitement), and, secondly, because most of them would have been of the view that they were about to enter the judgement of the afterlife, and that humble confessors would be less likely to burn for infinity than troublemakers to the end.

Given that most 'last dying speeches' of which we know were not far removed from the staged confessions of a Moscow court in the 1930s, it is quite remarkable that some such speeches were unchecked, uncensored and anticipative of the freer climate which would characterise the Tyburn area over a century after the last public hanging there in 1783.

One such recorded example is Hannah Blay, hanged in 1668 for her part in a murder. Advised by the clergymen who visited her in prison to repent for her crime and her sins, 'she would laugh at them', and, according to a contemporary account, 'ended her wicked life by a shameful death, without the least signs of repentance for her abominable whoredomes and wickedness'. Six years earlier, on 19 April 1662, Samuel Pepys noted in his *Diary* that whilst out shopping in Aldgate:

'I stood and did see Barkestead, Okey and Corbet drawne towards the gallows at Tiburne; and there they were hanged and Quarterd. They all looked very cheerfully. But I hear they all die defending what they did to the King to be just — which is very strange.'[3]

What they did to the King, Charles II, was attempt to kill him. Here were three men tried and executed for regicide, and yet even upon the gallows

3. R Latham and W Matthews (eds), *The Diary of Samuel Pepys*, Volume 3, London, 1970, p66.

two of them defended their position in public. (Pepys was misinformed in the case of Okey, who did indeed repent.) The significance of Pepys' observation is his surprise that men who had engaged in an activity as bold as regicide should have defended it in their gallows speech. JA Sharpe explains this discrepancy between the expected resistance to the last of the condemned and the tameness of the speeches published in the accounts of the various Ordinaries when he states that: 'Defiance at the gallows was unlikely to be permitted and even less likely to be reported.' This suggestion is supported by Linebaugh's research into the records of early eighteenth century 'last dying speeches':

'Eighteenth-century Sheriffs and Secretaries of State kept an attentive ear to these gallows' utterances, and were prompt to intervene when the words spoken might question the Hanoverian Succession, the doctrine of private property, the sovereignty of money or approved norms of sexual conduct.'[4]

When the Cato Street conspirators were executed (at Newgate rather than Tyburn, but the spectacle was before a large crowd), it proved impossible to prevent the condemned men from using the occasion for the purpose of revolutionary speech-making. The men, whose crime had been to plot the assassination of the Cabinet and the murder of a Bow Street police officer who had attempted to arrest them, went to the gallows sucking oranges and singing revolutionary songs. 'Oh! Give me Death or Liberty!', cried out James Inge, manifesting what the Ordinary reported as 'the most determined obduracy'.

How many Tyburn speeches went unreported or censored? How many scaffold rebels were cut off in mid-flow (rarely can the verb have been so literal)? How often would the crowds assemble at Tyburn in the hope that here, if nowhere else, the common man and woman might be allowed to voice their free opinion? These questions must remain matters of uncertainty, but we can be sure that long after the hangings moved from Tyburn to Newgate, and after the practice of the 'last dying speech' was no longer encouraged by officialdom, it was to Tyburn that the crowds returned to speak in a land where their voices were not supposed to be heard. The seeds of uncontrolled public discourse had been planted inadvertently around the Triple Tree at Tyburn, and, in conscious continuity or otherwise, it was to that corner of Hyde Park that the disenfranchised

4.   Linebaugh, op cit, pp88-91.

and publicly voiceless went in the nineteenth century when a place for open-air discussion was sought.

☆   ☆   ☆

In the summer of 1855 the crowds returned to Hyde Park, this time to speak for themselves rather than witness any pathetic gallows oratory. What occurred was described by *The Morning Post* as 'a scene, in the highest degree disgraceful and dangerous', and 'an outrage on law and decency'. The 'outrage' in question was the assembly of some hundred thousand people to oppose Lord Robert Grosvenor's Sunday Trading Bill. The meeting had been called by the rump of the London Chartists, with a key role being played by the working class poet, JB Leno. Handbills and posters circulated across London announced: 'An open-air meeting of artisans, workers and "the lower orders" generally... for three o'clock on the right bank of the Serpentine, on the side towards Kensington Gardens.'

Sir Robert Mayne, the Superintendent of the Metropolitan Police, issued a ban upon the gathering. The crowds gathered illegally. James Bligh, a Chartist, took the chair, immediately to be informed by Inspector Banks of the police that the park was the private property of the Crown and meetings could not be held there. Bligh attempted to defend his right to speak on the grounds that the park was a public space. He was arrested. A riot ensued. Of this clash between free speakers and the state, Karl Marx, who was present for the meeting, recorded somewhat over-excitedly that 'yesterday in Hyde Park the English revolution began'.[5]

On the following Sunday, 1 July, another attempt to hold an open-air meeting was made. It was preceded by the posting of police notices throughout London prohibiting any meetings in Hyde Park, or the gathering of any large numbers of people. According to police records, 150 000 people had arrived in Hyde Park by the time that the meeting was due to commence. An hour later Sir Robert Mayne, on horseback, supported by some 800 police officers, entered the meeting with the obvious intention of enforcing the ban with the use of truncheons. One hundred and four arrests were made, and large numbers were injured, one fatally. The bloody event was followed by the summoning of a 'Royal Commission to inquire into the alleged disturbances of the public peace in Hyde Park, Sunday, 1 July 1855; and the conduct of the Metropolitan Police in connection with the same'. Its report condemned the police handling of the meeting, and even reprimanded Mayne. More impor-

5. *Neue Oder-Zeitung*, 28 June 1855.

tantly, it reflected a growing ambivalence within the state authorities as to the wisdom of banning people from meeting in the open air to discuss their grievances. Although the government's Law Officers, Cockburn, Bethell and Willes, asserted the right of the state to exclude the public from the park, the political sagacity of applying the principle was left as a matter for some doubt.

The police violence did not discourage the novelty of public speaking in Hyde Park. Within months of the July riot, on 14 October a meeting in the park was addressed by a carpenter whose oratory was undisturbed by truncheons. He held another meeting the following Sunday, and congratulated the crowd for allowing free speech to be exercised in what he declared to be 'their own park'. By 18 November the police presence was being felt again, and, due to their intervention and the riotous outcome, no further meetings are known to have been held in Hyde Park until 1859, when it was decided to hold a meeting in support of Napoleon's Italian policy. Again, in 1862 a meeting was called in support of Garibaldi and the campaign for Italian unification. Mayne banned the meeting, but it was held, and, according to the *Morning Advertiser*, between 12 000 and 15 000 people attended it. Their presence resulted in the inevitable clash between police and populace.

It was in the year between the spring of 1866 and 1867 that the question of the freedom of people to gather in Hyde Park for the purpose of open political discussion was to come to a decisive head. The political atmosphere within which this occurred was the turmoil surrounding the reform of the franchise. The Liberal government's proposed Second Reform Bill offered too little to the radicals, including the well-organised and mainly working class Reform League, and too much to obtain the support of the conservative Whigs whose disaffection brought down the Russell-Gladstone Administration. This was replaced by a minority Conservative government led by Derby in the Lords and Disraeli in the Commons.

The Reform League called a meeting to be held in Hyde Park on 2 July 1866. Mayne at first banned it, but then, perhaps mindful of the fact that he was dealing with an organisation of 600 branches, he relented, and a meeting of approximately 50 000 people was addressed by the league's President, Beales, as well as other speakers. Another meeting was called for 23 July. Mayne was determined that it should not be held, but, still smarting from his censure after the 1855 riot, he felt impotent to issue a prohibition without the collaboration of the government. This was obtained with no difficulty from the newly-appointed Home Secretary, Spencer Walpole, a politician seeking to carve a reputation as a defender of public order. A ban upon 'meetings for the purpose of delivering or hearing speeches, or for the public discussion of popular and exciting topics' was issued.

The Reform League was not by any means a revolutionary body. The inclination of its leadership was to comply with the ban. Charles Bradlaugh, by then one of its most prominent and crowd-drawing orators, pleaded with the leadership to resist the ban. The policy finally adopted was one of typical English compromise (cum-retreat): it was agreed that the meeting would assemble at Hyde Park, but when confronted by the police the speakers would agree to go to Trafalgar Square, taking the audience with them, and so diffusing the threat of disorder.

The meeting, being organised for a Monday, was due to commence at 7pm. When the crowds arrived they found the park surrounded by 1700 police, mainly at the gates. Beales and his fellow leaders arrived by cab, observed the police presence, announced the change of venue to Trafalgar Square, and proceeded there to address a not very well attended meeting. Most of their 'followers' had not followed them, but remained at Hyde Park. Within a short time the police were outnumbered by a determined crowd intending to assemble and discuss. The force of the crowd broke down the park railings and secured free access. This was far from being an act of mere vandalism, as was noted by Cowper, the former First Commissioner of Works, who reported that, while the crowd 'forced down the railings and made good their entrance to the Park, they abstained from injuring the flowers, and even in the heat and hurry of the disturbance, they frequently went round along the grass so as not to tread upon the flower-beds and borders'. Mayne called for military support. A regiment of Life Guards was given the duty of protecting the police against the anger of the crowd, some of whom were throwing stones at them. The park entrances were defended by five companies of Coldstream Guards. None of this prevented speeches from being made and politics from being discussed in the open air — a harmless activity, one might think. The speeches given in front of one of the trees drew the largest audience; it was subsequently to be known as Reformers' Tree, and it was there that Donald Soper was to speak regularly for six decades of the following century.

The behaviour of the police was reported by the *Morning Star*, which accused them of striking out indiscriminately:

'... with their truncheons like savages who, having been under temporary control, were now at full liberty to break heads and cut open faces to their hearts' content. It mattered not to them whether the interloper had actively exerted himself to force an entrance, or whether he had been merely hurled in the irresistible crush of those who pressed behind. Wherever there was a skull to fracture, they did their best to fracture it; everybody was in their eyes an enemy to whom no mercy was to be shown.'

By midnight of 23 July the crowds were cleared from Hyde Park. Some hours earlier Beales had concluded his anaemic performance in another part of central London. The crowds left, but they returned the next day, and for two days after that. Homes of the rich and powerful which surrounded the park were attacked and sometimes entered; even the Prime Minister, Lord Derby, was to complain in parliament that the windows of his domestic abode had been broken. JS Mill recorded that he had to plead with the leaders of the League to avoid a revolutionary conflict arising in Hyde Park, a somewhat overstated fear. On Wednesday, 25 July Beales visited Walpole at the Home Office to negotiate peace. It was agreed that the League would clear the park of the crowds so contemptuously described by Gladstone as 'the scum of the people'. The only concession that Walpole made to Beales was the promise that the government Law Officers would be called upon to issue a judgement as to whether it was rightful to exclude the people from the park. (This was hardly much of a concession, as Walpole had already called for the ruling before Beales came to the Home Office.) On Friday, 28 July, after a Cabinet discussion of the Hyde Park affair, statements were made in both Houses. According to the account in *The Annual Register* of 1866:

'The conduct of the Government, and especially the Secretary of State for the Home Department, underwent some unfavourable criticism... Earl Granville asked the Prime Minister whether he would order to be laid before Parliament a copy of the instructions issued to the military and the police, and also inquired what measures had been taken to prevent a repetition of the recent disorders.'

On Saturday, 28 July matters grew worse for Walpole. The Law Officers decided that it was 'impractical' to deny people the liberty to meet in the park. As to the question of whether those holding the meeting had asked the government's permission to do so, the Law Officers reiterated: 'In our Opinion there is not for any practical Purpose a legal Authority to disperse by Force a Meeting of the kind supposed, consisting of a large number of persons, and that whether Notice has or has not been given.'[6] This was unequivocal. But still, when in April of the following year, after a winter of rising unemployment, increasing bread prices and an outbreak of cholera in the metropolis, the Reform League called a meeting to be held in Hyde Park on 6 May, Walpole's instant response was a ban, issued on 1 May. The ban was backed up by the appointment of 12 000 special constables to defend the park on the day, together with all the police and military force necessary. Every indication from the Home Office threatened the most violent repression: little less than a London Peterloo.

The debate on the forthcoming Hyde Park meeting which was held in the House of Commons on 3 May, and which was reported *verbatim* in *Hansard*, illuminated the fears of the government and the level of defence of free speech by the small minority of parliamentarians who opposed the ban. At a time when the principal business of parliament was the reform of the franchise on the basis of a property qualification, here was a debate concerning the liberties associated with unqualified, uncontrolled, non-governmental democracy.

Opening the debate, John Bright drew 'the attention of the House to the proposed interference of the government with the public meeting in Hyde Park'. There had been several other Reform meetings held outdoors, he explained, in Glasgow, Edinburgh, Leeds and Birmingham, the latter attracting some quarter of a million attendees. These had passed peacefully. Indeed, there was no reason to believe that 'great public meetings have been attended with breaches of the peace in this country'. He went on:

'One of the most signal instances of a breach of the peace was in 1819, in Manchester, where men met to ask for Reform and for a repeal of the Corn Laws. If there had been no interference with that meeting it would have been as tranquil as we are in this House at this moment. But because it was interfered with by blind, bigoted, foolish magistrates... there was a breach of the peace and bloodshed.'

To appoint thousands of special constables from the middle class, to regard a meeting for reform as an act of menace, was 'one of the most insane things that any Home Secretary or magistrate could do'. So, what ought he to do? 'To offer no kind of opposition to the peaceful entrance of the people into the Park, and when they are in the Park, to take no

6. Law Officers' Report by Cairns and Bovill, 28 July 1888.

part whatever in endeavouring to prevent... the intended proceedings of the day.'

This was clearly a challenge to Walpole to lift the ban. Not surprisingly, Walpole failed to accept it. He rested his case in the Commons upon 'the right of the Crown to the Royal Parks, and as consequent on that right, the power either to permit certain things to be done, or the power to prohibit certain other things from being done'. Political discussion in parks was one of those things which ought to be prohibited. Walpole explained his reasoning for this:

'In almost all... parks they make it a condition... that they shall not be open for two purposes – namely, purposes either of political or religious discussions. The reason is obvious. These are two topics on which men's minds are easily excited, and on which contrary opinions may be brought to bear in an adverse manner. If you opened the parks for the discussion of one set of opinions, you must open them for that of the other set of opinions.'

Such an 'obvious' objection to democratic debate in public having been asserted, Walpole went on to explain how it was easy to prevent 'small bodies of men' from entering parks for the purpose of preaching and discussion: 'If they resist, you can deal with them for a breach of the peace.' The problem with the forthcoming meeting was its size, making it more difficult to silence the debate. The League had been informed: 'If they simply wished to have a meeting for the discussion of the question of Reform in the open air, in order to avoid the expense of an indoor meeting, Primrose Hill was open to them for that purpose.' But if they entered Hyde Park in contravention of the government ban, this would constitute 'an act of trespass'.

William Gladstone was quite clear that there should be no party differences on this matter: 'Upon questions of this kind the space that separates the two sides of this House entirely disappears. There can be but one sentiment in any quarter of this House with regard to the paramount importance and sacredness... of public order.' The existence of 'permanent agitation' would be 'a great public evil', and the government must be supported as 'administrators of the law for the sake of the law itself and for the sake of the public interest'.

The supporters of the government prohibition exhibited more fear than reason. Mr Neate said that the government had shown 'singular forbearance' towards 'these agitators' whose wish to meet was an insult to the House of Commons, which was there to debate the political affairs of the nation. Mr Davenport-Bromley feared that the proposed Hyde Park meeting would lead to a riot, and he reported from a friend living near to the park (in Cumberland Gate) that his windows and nearly all of his furniture had been destroyed the previous July, and 'he did not look forward to next Monday with any feelings of satisfaction'. Mr Otway 'expressed an opinion that Hyde Park was not at all a suitable place for holding political meetings', and wanted it made clear what the government intended to do if people ignored the ban and entered the park, 'whether the government meant to take forcible means to eject them, or whether they would be allowed to continue the discussion'. Captain Hayter was quite clear that forcible means should be used, preferably 'a special force of cavalry and infantry to prevent the people from going into the park'. After all: 'If the people were once allowed to enter the park, then the difficulty would arise of driving them out again, and the utmost danger might result, not only to property but to person.' Mr Selwyn announced to the House that he had been a special constable in 1848, when the government had been afraid of the Chartist gathering at Kennington Common, and he was ready to serve again in that capacity. If the people wanted a meeting they should go to Primrose Hill, where there would not be 'the same likelihood of damage being inflicted upon the houses in the neighbourhood as was the case in Hyde Park', but it was quite obvious to him that 'Hyde Park had been chosen as the place of meeting simply for the purpose of intimidation'. Mr Denman, also a special constable in 1848, offered his services again if he could be of any use. The atmosphere of the House bordered on panic.

There were a few lone voices of dissent. Mr Kinnaid said that he had no strong feelings on the meeting himself, but thought it should be known by the House that the people of Perth had written to urge him to state that they were in favour of a meeting being held in Hyde Park the following Monday. Mr Whalley was of the view that if bans were going to be placed upon radical gatherings, they could also apply to 'reviews and other public celebrations'. Apart from Bright's, the only coherent speech in opposition to the ban came from Mr PA Taylor, who said that the people were distinctly in the right in holding a meeting:

'The government did not believe that the proceedings of the Reform League would cause a disturbance. The only disturbance to be apprehended was through Government interference with the meeting, and hence any responsibility for breach of the peace would rest with the Government.'

As they made their way to Hyde Park on 6 May, the tens of thousands of men and women seeking to assemble in the face of the direst state threats might well have sensed the atmosphere of the procession from Newgate to Tyburn a century earlier. That the gathering would take place without lives being lost was something that few would predict.

The announced intention of the government was motivated by fear, and so was its failure to implement its threat. Both Walpole for the government and Mayne for the police knew that the policy of prohibition could only work if it succeeded in frightening people into non-attendance. This did not happen: upwards of 150 000 people arrived at Hyde Park for the meeting. Both police and troops stood impassively as the government ban was ignored. If Peterloo was the moment of unquestionable defeat for working class free speech, the Hyde Park meeting of May 1867 was the occasion of dignified triumph. The forces of the state retreated. The transformation of a place of working class execution into one of workers' elocution — from death confessions to free discussions — was underway. All that was left was for the state authorities to recognise the new situation.

Walpole resigned as Home Secretary the next morning. Queen Victoria, saddened by her government's humiliation at the hands of her subjects, wrote to sympathise with her ex-Minister. The Conservative Party was shocked by the government's retreat; the Carlton Club had written to Disraeli emphasising that there must be no capitulation. But Captain Hayter had been right: the people, once having asserted their right to assemble and discuss freely in the park, were not prepared to go away after the meeting and leave the space to their masters. More meetings followed. May 1867 saw the beginning of a new kind of institution in British political culture: a place where any person or organisation may go to speak without permission to those wanting freely to listen.

In 1872 the Parks Regulation Act was passed. It limited the right of the police within the park to the maintenance of civil order, but to play no role in granting permission for meetings to be held or determining what may be spoken about within meetings. Certain regulations which have evolved since then are still in effect: speakers' platforms must be a sufficient distance from one another so as not to allow one orator to shout down the voice of another; literature cannot be sold at meetings, and collections may not be called for (although both of these regulations are broken regularly); speakers are confined to what is legally known as 'the speaking area' (Speakers' Corner); and it is forbidden to impart racing tips from the platform. Other than this, speakers are constrained by laws relating to slander, obscenity, blasphemy and the incitement of racial hatred. In general these have proved to be more technical constraints than enforced ones.

The liberalism which seems to pervade the post-1872 status of Speakers' Corner is, like much liberal imagery, rather deceptive. From the earliest conflicts concerning democratic liberties, there have always been those who have seen more sense in allowing 'the masses' (as the non-elite is perceived) to have a measure of tolerated autonomy. Even in the debate in parliament in 1866 on the suppression of the July meeting of that year, the Chancellor of the Exchequer, Gladstone, was of the view that 'parks were unfit places for political meetings' in that 'the scum of this great city would take advantage of such an assemblage', and yet this did not deter him from seeing the value of public meetings in general, for he believed them to be 'a valuable political safety-valve'. The notion of 'a little bit of free speech' as a harmless eccentricity, illuminating both the ill-informed self-opinionation of autodidactic demagogues and the democratic credentials of the tolerating state, is one that has been embraced, consciously or otherwise, by more than a few adherents to essentially elitist conceptions of democracy. Just as later TV bosses were to see the case for letting the odd rebel have an access slot along with the misunderstood and the transparently crazy, so the sneering condescension of a Voltairean defence unto the last of the freedom to shout at Speakers' Corner has become one of the less attractive characteristics of conservative English self-satisfaction. In his essay 'Britain is a Democracy', informed by the acute theoretical insight of Roland Barthes, Gilbert Adair writes of 'the ideological polyphony, the sheer Babel of voices confronting the casual spectator' at Speakers' Corner, all appearing to assert the same message: that Britain is a democracy. This function of democratic spectacle serves to immunise onlookers against the more profoundly real recognition of eroded democratic values. Adair suggests that through this spectacle 'the state is seen to have established its credentials as a defender of free speech; for, by a paradox familiar, and dear to the governments of Western democracies, nothing more surely attests to freedom of speech as a political reality than the fact of an individual publicly (freely) alleging that it has been muzzled'. Adair is right to declare caution against the fraudulent appropriation by the political authorities of democratic customs which they have historically resisted. The pertinence of the essay's concluding passage is worthy of note:

'No one would take issue with the unified "consensus" of Speakers' Corner: Britain is a democracy. But, with a country which, more frequently than any other, has been brought before the European Court for having violated certain basic human rights, which vindictively avenges every infringement of the Official Secrets Act..., which is contriving to secure a virtual monopoly in the flow of information, the danger is that such institutions as the BBC (with its appointees vetted by MI5) and the national press (ever-increasingly the private property of a handful of staunchly reactionary "barons") could find themselves transformed into equivalently peripheral and innocuous showcases of political independence... Freedom of speech on a soapbox may also come to resemble nothing so much as a statue on its plinth; and statues, as the ultimate stage of rigor mortis, tend to be erected to the dead.'[7]

Less subtle critics have asserted that Speakers' Corner is a charade: a mockery of democracy; a ritualised public spectacle representing a living monument to the trickery of 'bourgeois democracy'. That such critiques have not infrequently been offered over the years by people who have unflinchingly defended the democratic integrity of Stalin's 1936 Constitution, and whose conception of public discussion expands no further than leaders shouting slogans through megaphones, does not testify to their capacity to judge the health of a democratic culture. Unlike those 'invented traditions' explored by Hobsbawm *et al* – in reality, cultural fabrications of a counterfactual history – Speakers' Corner is a tradition with an unusual cultural authenticity, part of which stems from the blood-saturated ground upon which it stands, and part from the often forgotten history of resistance out of which it emerged and has survived.

7.   G Adair, *Myths and Memories*, London, 1986, p83.

The Age of Discussion: Fears and Images

IN 1872, the year that parliament legislated for unfettered freedom of speech in Hyde Park, Walter Bagehot, the conservative constitutionalist, wrote a book in which he referred to his own time as the 'Age of Discussion'. Motivated by an evolutionist perspective which owed much to Darwin and to Spencer, Bagehot perceived that the rule of custom and prejudice had given way to that of debated public choices. But Bagehot was too much of a reactionary to regard such a development with neutrality. In recognising this rupture of 'the yoke of fixed custom', Bagehot sets before the readers of his *Physics and Politics* a cautionary observation:

'As far as it goes, the mere putting up of a subject to discussion, with the object of being guided by that discussion, is a clear admission that the subject is in no degree settled by established rule, and that men are free to choose in it. It is an admission too that there is no sacred authority – no one transcendent and divinely appointed man whom in that matter the community is bound to obey. And if a single subject or group of subjects be once admitted to discussion, ere long the habit of discussion comes to be established, the sacred charm of use and wont to be dissolved. "Democracy", it has been said in modern times, "is like the grave; it takes, but it does not give." The same is true of "discussion". Once effectually submit a subject to that ordeal, and you can never withdraw it again; you can never clothe it with mystery, or fence it by consecration; it remains for ever open to free choice, and exposed to profane deliberation.'[1]

The sense of floodgates having burst open is very clear. Bagehot, with an honesty of expression not exhibited by all of his conservative contemporaries, was quite right to connect this unstoppable process of 'profane deliberation' to the question of the viability of democracy. If equality in the right to vote meant equality in the liberty to speak and be listened to, Bagehot and his fellow conservatives could only subscribe to such a free-

1. W Bagehot, *Physics and Politics*, London, 1872, p94.

dom as a point of constitutional fiction. In reality, they were deeply dubious as to the value of being governed by the consequences of uncontrolled popular discussion, and, furthermore, they entertained undisguised suspicion of the vulgar informality of autonomous discussion amongst those who came to be labelled as 'the masses'.

The masses, as this collectivity of votes with chattering voices was labelled by Carlyle as early as 1839, were the late Victorian inheritors of the 'swinish multitude' of the seventeenth century, and the 'mob' of the eighteenth century. The new and highly significant characteristic which qualified the sneering description was that now the erstwhile rabble had power not only to determine who would govern it, but to make audible the conditions upon which it would consent to be governed. Democracy and Demos were inseparable; deliberation would henceforth precede decision; the masses would not only speak but be heard.

The capacity of the masses to say anything worth hearing was a matter for the most profound doubt amongst the intellectual elite. Hardly had the platforms been erected in the parks and on the street corners than a new and highly influential socio-psychology of mass behaviour made its first appearance.

The founding document of this critique of the masses was Gustave Le Bon's *The Crowd: A Study of the Popular Mind*, first published in French in 1895. (It was translated into English a year later, and went into 15 impressions between then and 1925.) Le Bon's aim was to examine a new social phenomenon:

'Organised crowds have always played an important part in the life of peoples, but this part has never been of such moment as at present. The substitution of the unconscious action of crowds for the conscious activity of individuals is one of the principal characteristics of the present age.'[2]

The entire tenor of Le Bon's introductory chapter, 'The Era of Crowds', is one of fear. The gaining of the vote by large numbers of (male) workers was not the principal threat. 'It is by association that crowds have come to procure ideas with respect to their interests', warns Le Bon, and as a result 'have arrived at a consciousness of their strength.' The ultimate effect of this mass confidence will be 'nothing less than a determination utterly to destroy society as it now exists, with a view to making it hark

2.   G Le Bon, *The Crowd: A Study of the Popular Mind*, London, 1922, p18.

back to that primitive communism which was the normal condition of all human groups before the dawn of civilisation'. For Le Bon the crowd represented a force for the decomposition of all that he cherished: civilised property values and authority from above. What does Le Bon say about crowds? To begin with, he regards the crowd as a product of psychology rather than numbers: 'A thousand individuals accidentally gathered in a public place without any determined object in no way constitute a crowd from the psychological point of view.' The crowd descends into the masses when its members have lost their conscious personalities, and have acquired 'certain provisional but determinable general characteristics', which Le Bon proceeds to describe. Mass crowds are impulsive, irritable, credulous, suggestible, intolerant and, above all, irrational, 'being only capable of thinking in images'. A member of a crowd 'is no longer conscious of his acts'. Crowd members, who hover perpetually 'on the borderland of unconsciousness, readily yielding to all suggestions, having all the violence of feeling peculiar to beings who cannot appeal to the influence of reason, deprived of all critical faculty, cannot be otherwise than excessively credulous'. The oratory which might appeal to the mindless masses of Le Bon's imagination is hardly likely to be directed towards the rational intellect. Indeed, Le Bon notes, with a sweeping observation, that:

'An orator wishing to move a crowd must make an abusive use of violent affirmations. To exaggerate, to affirm, to resort to repetitions, and never attempt to prove anything by reasoning are methods of argument well known to speakers at public meetings.'[3]

Without the slightest attempt to differentiate between one public meeting and another, or amongst the variety of interests which might be under discussion, Le Bon goes on to assert dogmatically:

'A chain of logical argumentation is totally incomprehensible to crowds, and for this reason it is permissible to say that they do not reason or that they reason falsely, and are not to be influenced by reasoning. Astonishment is felt at times on reading certain speeches at their weakness, and yet they had an enormous influence on the crowds which listened to them; but it is forgotten that they were intended to persuade collectivities, and not to be read by philosophers. An orator in intimate communication

3.   Ibid, p57.

with a crowd can evoke images by which it will be seduced. If he is successful his object has been attained, and 20 volumes of harangues... are not worth the few phrases which appealed to the brains it was required to convince.'[4]

There is a striking similarity between this and the reflection by Hitler in *Mein Kampf* that 'the great mass of people consists neither of professors nor of diplomats', and 'confine their perceptive faculties to the realm of feeling'; therefore: 'He who wishes to win the broad mass must know the key which opens the door to its heart.'[5] Hitler had read the German translation of Le Bon's *magnus opus*. Le Bon's analysis of crowd behaviour was eccentric and remote from the experience of British public meetings. Indeed, it would be of little significance were it not the main theoretical foundation of a theory of fear of vocally-active crowds which was to influence other popular works and affect the imagery surrounding free speech. In 1901 the criminologist, Gabriel Tarde, published his *Opinion and the Crowd* in which he emphasised the tendency towards imitative behaviour within crowds. Graham Wallas' *Human Nature in Politics*, first published in 1908, examined the gullibility of the political masses, and the susceptibility of crowds to be manipulated by calculating oligarchies. In 1916 Wilfred Trotter's *Instincts of the Herd in Peace and War* had an effect upon the political thinking of both Mussolini in Italy, who rated it on a par with the fascistic philosophy of Gentile, and Ramsay MacDonald, the British Labour leader. Trotter's imagery of the instinctive suggestibility of crowds related to the prevalent pessimism of an age in which sentiments of prewar international working class solidarity had given way to the barbarism of the trenches. In 1921 Freud praised Le Bon's 'brilliant psychological character-sketch of the group mind',[6] and this marked the commencement of his outspoken contempt for the ideal of mass human rationality which culminated in 1929 with the publication of *Civilisation and Its Discontents*. Before then came yet another major contributor to the intellectual cult of the malleable and rationally impotent masses, José Ortega y Gasset's *The Revolt of the Masses*, published in 1930, a work reflecting a fear of the unwanted intrusion of the crowd into areas, both geographical and intellectual, where they could only ever be confused and disappointed. The connecting element amongst the theorists of the

4. Ibid, p74.
5. A Hitler, *Mein Kampf*, Munich, 1936, p371.
6. S Freud, *Group Psychology and the Analysis of the Ego*, original 1921, English translation London, 1940.

masses was a fear that the democratic appropriation of the rationalist promise of the Enlightenment would conflict with human nature, that is to say, the inherent behaviour of workers gathered together. Were such beings capable of entering into reasoned discourse? Le Bon, here again prefiguring Hitler almost to the word, offers no optimism in answering this question: 'Crowds are only cognisant of simple and extreme sentiments; the opinions, ideas, and beliefs suggested to them are accepted or rejected as a whole, and considered as absolute truths or as not less absolute errors.'

Given such an allegedly simple-minded approach to deliberation, it is hardly surprising that, in Le Bon's view, 'crowds... are quick to act'. It is this impulsive tendency to arrive at conclusions which most worried conservative ideologists, comfortable in their own Burkean methodology of gradual thought. The same anxiety concerned Bagehot in his consideration of the Age of Discussion: 'An inability to stay quiet, an irritable desire to act directly, is one of the most conspicuous failings of mankind.' This preference for quietism was hardly new in the history of elitist responses to free speech. Bagehot is quite preoccupied with it, stating that 'we should have been a far wiser race than we are if we had been readier to sit quiet'. Scientific achievements, contends Bagehot, were the products of 'sedentary, quiet, thinking people'. Indeed, such advances would have come sooner had it not been for those exhibiting 'irritable activity', and 'the "wish to be doing something"'. Philanthropists, whose efforts Bagehot fears might be in conflict with the principle of natural selection, are examples of people consumed by 'a wild passion for instant action', as are revolutionaries: 'There is an excessive energy in revolutions if there is such energy anywhere.' It is to Bagehot's credit that his analysis can be distinguished from those of the critics of the masses who come after him, with their caricatured sociological depictions of crowds, and little but fear as conclusions from their observations; one has in mind here Elias Canetti's *Crowds And Power*, and Serge Moscovici's *The Age of the Crowd*. Unlike these more recent crowd theorists, Bagehot does attempt to offer a remedy to the dangers perceived in the Age of Discussion:

'If you want to stop instant and immediate action, always make it a condition that the action shall not begin till a considerable number of persons have talked over it, and have agreed on it. If those persons be people of different temperaments, different ideas, and different educations, you have an almost infallible security that nothing, or almost nothing, will be done with excessive rapidity. Each kind of persons will have their

45

spokesman; each spokesman will have his characteristic objection, and each his characteristic counter-proposition, and so in the end nothing will probably be done, or at least only the minimum which is plainly urgent.'[7]

There is a political elegance in this quietist, conservative recipe for talking and then probably doing nothing. Its emphasis upon class consensus and its unstated assumption that if the lesser orders must discuss social affairs they should do so in the presence of higher minds succeed in offering what might be regarded as a policy of containment for the Age of Discussion. That it was written within a year of the passage of the Education Act, making elementary state education compulsory for the first time, and within four years of the first votes being granted to significant numbers of artisans, is hardly coincidental; it is indicative of an age in which, recognising that these threatening masses could not be excluded from discussion, it was seen as prudent to provide them with their own humble Speakers' Corner to sound off in. The fear of uncouth and riotous working class discussion bore little resemblance to the reality of public, mainly open-air, meetings which proliferated in the late Victorian and Edwardian decades. To begin with, 'the masses', so prominent in sociological and literary depiction of free speech, were an invention, a fictitious label for those excluded from the university debating societies and self-proclaimed intelligentsia.

John Carey, in his magisterial account *The Intellectuals and The Masses*, rightly observes:

'The mass... is a metaphor for the unknowable and invisible. We cannot see the mass. Crowds can be seen; but the mass is the crowd in its metaphysical aspect — the sum of all possible crowds — and that can take on conceptual form only as metaphor. The metaphor of the mass serves the purpose of individual self-assertion because it turns other people into a conglomerate. It denies them the individuality which we ascribe to ourselves and to people we know.'[8]

Those who write of 'the masses being easily swayed' never include themselves, or their readers, within the masses. The term is a codified reference to the excluded, uneducated, unprivileged and unimportant — and, of course, all of these adjectives contain their own loaded ideological as-

7. Bagehot, op cit, p194.
8. J Carey, *The Intellectuals and The Masses: Pride and Prejudice Amongst the Literary Intelligentsia, 1880-1939*, London, 1992, p21.

sumptions. Even the soapbox, the symbolic image of the humble meeting, is a myth; very few street or park orators actually spoke from wooden boxes. Outdoor speakers usually stood upon specially constructed platforms, with the name of their topic or organisation painted on the front and steps at the back, allowing for a dignified ascension to a stage of between one and two square feet. In the absence of a platform, speakers would often stand upon mounds or boxes. (Donald Soper's first meeting at Tower Hill in 1926 was held with him standing on a wall.) But the flimsy image of the soapbox fails to recognise the self-respect and dignity which characterised most public oratory.

Equally false is the patronising image of the public meeting as a mere spectacle or ranting performance. This image derives from the failure of observers, often from the distance of academia, to recognise the interactive nature of meetings. Most accounts of public meetings ignore the most common kind of street or park gathering, and concentrate upon mass rallies and pre-planned demonstrations. Indeed, meetings such as that in St Peter's Fields, Manchester in 1819 would have fitted into this latter category had it not been for the interaction between the crowd and the militia which turned it into a massacre. Most public meetings did not involve audiences coming to listen to planned speeches by famous orators whose words could not be challenged.

The average open-air meeting would involve a speaker and a group of supporters carrying a platform to an established spot, usually referred to as a speaking station, where they would proceed to erect the platform. Many speaking stations attracted more than one platform per evening, or during the day at weekends, so it was important to set up the platform far enough away from other platforms to avoid speakers' voices from being drowned out by one another. Anecdotes are told of speakers arriving hours before the commencement of a meeting in order to establish their platform at the most advantageous point of the park or pavement. Starting a meeting was a specialist skill, usually performed by a chairman. (This role was not uncommonly performed by women speakers, but the term prevailed.) Drawing a crowd to a meeting involved oratorical techniques unknown to 'professional' orators whose audiences had been brought in especially to hear them. In the cases of political or religious organisations with their own publications, regular lists of outdoor meeting stations and speakers were printed, but these were mainly to remind supporters where and when to attend, rather than to advertise the meetings to potential audience members. The success of meetings in attracting and keeping a crowd was determined by the capacity of speakers to catch the attention of passers-by, and contingent factors such as the weather and the presence or otherwise of hecklers. Very few platform speakers (though there were some) could build a crowd simply on the basis of un-interrupted oration; it was the ability of a speaker to respond with fast wit and knowledge to questioners and hecklers which sustained a big crowd.

From the moment of its 'revival' in the 1880s, the socialist movement recognised the importance of open-air propaganda. Even before organised socialist bodies were formed a number of radical clubs, as well as the National Secular Society, had seen the need to take their messages to the streets and parks. They pursued this course with vigour: the Manhood Suffrage League's open-air meetings in Seven Dials and Cumberland Market in the mid-1870s were an important means of connecting the of-ten dry didactic discourse of the lecture hall with the wider interests of working class people. The most popular of the secularist street preachers was Jesse Cocks of the Stratford Secular Society in East London, who spoke also as an Owenite socialist and organiser for the First Interna-tional. Once the Social Democratic Federation was formed in 1883, even its Eton-educated and rather arrogant leader, Henry Myers Hyndman, condescended to address the workers, although he concedes in his autobi-ography that he found the task 'most trying':

'At first I had... a strong prejudice against addressing the hopeless sort of audiences we had to deal with... I always consider I first stripped myself of my class prejudices when I addressed a gathering largely made up of rather debauched-looking persons round the old pump at Clerkenwell Green. I laughed a little at myself standing there in the full rig-out of the well-to-do fashionable, holding forth to these manifest degenerates on the curse of capitalism and the glories of the coming time.'[9]

Despite Hyndman's evident lack of empathy for the crowd, and the al-ienating form in which he seems to have addressed them, he and his SDF comrades do seem to have made an impact by establishing these counter-pulpits to those of the established orthodoxy. Indeed, Hyndman himself came to recognise that there was 'no better training... for dealing with interruptions and attacks and questions than a course of street-corner oratory'.[10]

The SDF's contribution to open-air public discussion should not be

9.   HM Hyndman, *The Record of an Adventurous Life*, London, 1911, p341.
10. Ibid, p342.

confined to the rather arrogant posturing of its well-to-do leaders. As Martin Crick has argued in his useful history of the SDF, organised Marxian socialism in the 1880s amounted to rather more than Hyndman and his clique, and is best studied in the provinces. For example, Willie Nairn, the pioneer Glaswegian SDF activist, was frequently to be heard declaring the case for socialism on Glasgow Green, where he was known as 'the professor' (he was a stonemason by occupation), and his contemporary, Bob Hutcheson, a shoemaker, was generally regarded as the most appealing of the SDF orators, capable of moving crowds that were comprised of all sorts of people.[11]

William Morris, the poet, designer and socialist, regarded the outdoor platform as the most important means of communicating ideas to the working class. At one of his first committee meetings as a member of the SDF (from which he resigned later that year), Morris endorsed the view of one Comrade Rowland who contended that 'street preaching' was the most important work to be undertaken by socialists. On 21 July 1884 Morris and other members of the Socialist League spoke from a cart with a red flag upon it at the Hyde Park rally organised by the Liberals in favour of an extended franchise. The socialists failed to gain much of an audience until one of the speakers, John Burns, made 'a contemptuous reference to John Bright', the Liberal speaker at the rally. According to Morris' account, this comment led to 'a storm of hooting in the audience', and a suggestion, not acted upon by the crowd, to throw Burns into the Serpentine. Perhaps it was this which led to Morris' nervousness about taking the platform in Hyde Park; on 15 June 1886 he wrote to his daughter of how he and other members of the Socialist League had spoken at Dorking where 'we were taken for a detachment of the Salvation Army' the day after having spoken at Hyde Park: 'I was quite nervous about it, I don't know why... we had a very quiet and good audience, and sold four quires of *Commonweal*; and I spoke twice, the second time not at all nervously.' Standing on a platform before a crowd of people who were not present with the specific intention of listening to what one has to say is an understandable cause for anxiety. Such a feeling is well expressed in Morris's poem, *The Pilgrims of Hope*, when he describes his initiation into the life of propaganda:

So I began the business, and in street-corners I spake
To knots of men. Indeed, that made my very heart ache,

11. M Crick, *The History of the Social Democratic Federation*, Keele, 1994.

So hopeless it seemed; for some stood by like men of wood;
And some, though fain to listen, but a few words understood;
And some but hooted and jeered: but whiles across some I came
Who were keen and eager to hear; as in dry flax the flame
So the quick thought flickered amongst them: and that indeed was a
feast.[12]

In his *Socialist Diary* of 1887 Morris gave an account of an outdoor meeting at Beadon Road in Hammersmith where he spoke for an hour to an audience of about 100 people:

'This audience characteristic of small open-air meetings also quite mixed, from labourers on their Sunday lounge to "respectable" people coming from church: the latter inclined to grin: the working men listening attentively trying to understand, but mostly failing to do so: a fair cheer when I ended, of course led by the three or four branch members present.'[13]

Most open-air meetings were of this undramatic nature. In such circumstances the presence of a heckling opponent could make a meeting, just as the presence of a drunk could break one. Occasionally, more exciting interventions occurred. Since its formation the SDF had been running street corner meetings at the junction of Dod Street and Burdett Road in Limehouse, East London. The police decided to regard such meetings as an act of obstruction – a legal judgement which seems to be almost entirely at the discretion of the police. Speakers were told to end the meetings, refused to do so, and were arrested. Fines were imposed upon speakers, and when Jack Williams refused to pay his, the court sentenced him to a month's hard labour. A Vigilance Committee was established to safeguard the use of the streets for meetings. On Sunday, 20 September 1885 a meeting in defence of free speech was held in Dod Street, and Morris was one of the speakers. The meeting itself passed peacefully, but as the crowd dispersed the police charged in, arresting two men who had been holding a banner, and injuring others. The next morning eight members of the crowd appeared at the Thames Police court, charged with causing an obstruction or resisting arrest. The presiding magistrate, Saunders, expressed a distinct unease at the report of such meetings being held on the East End streets, and proceeded to impose £2 fines upon seven of the men, and a sentence of two months hard labour upon the eighth, a tailor

12. *Three Works by William Morris*, London, 1983, p143.
13. F Boos (ed), *William Morris' Socialist Diary*, London, 1982, p27.

called Lyons. The outcry in the court was such that the police arrested Morris, who was brought before Saunders later the same day, and then released when it transpired that he was a famous poet. The following Sunday the socialists ran a peaceful and undisturbed meeting in Dod Street. A correspondent to the *Daily News* observed that the police action at Dod Street 'has caused more obstruction and disturbance than 12 months of socialistic lecturing'. It was clear that public feeling was disposed in favour of street corner oratory.

The following summer a number of cases of police attempts to break up socialist meetings were reported. On 31 July Morris wrote an article in *Commonweal*, the journal of the Socialist League, in which he commented on the 'arrogant petty tyranny' of the police: 'They would clear the streets of costermongers, organs, processions and lecturers of all kinds, and make them a sort of decent prison corridors, with people just trudging to and from their work.'[14] This was published only a week after Morris himself had appeared in court on a charge of obstruction after being arrested for speaking for half an hour on the socialist platform in Bell Street, off the Edgware Road.

The persecution of open-air speaking persisted. In 1888 a citizens' petition, mainly inspired by the shopkeeping middle class, called for a ban on Sunday meetings in Victoria Park, Hackney 'because of the bad, seditious, blasphemous and disgusting language used'. It failed, but a bye-law prohibiting the taking of collections at meetings in the park was passed. In his memoirs, Ralph Fox recalled how shopkeepers attempted to drive away the socialist platform from St Ann's Corner 'in the heart of a drab slum area' of Tottenham; on one occasion they hired a brass band to drown out the speaker's voice.[15]

Reports of outbreaks of rioting and uncouth disturbances at street or park meetings in the 1880s are not to be found. Even police records of these events contain no such descriptions; most crowds at meetings were found to be attentive and intelligently critical. The main disturbances were initiated by the police, reflecting a notion of order which came from those above them, and which had little meaning in the context of social reality.

The most dramatic and violent occurrence at a British open-air meeting took place on 13 November 1887. It has become known as 'Bloody Sunday'. This was no Le Bonist outburst of animalistic aggression on the

14. Cited in N Salmon (ed), *The Political Writings of William Morris*, Bristol, 1995, pp168-72.
15. R Fox, *Smoky Crusade*, London, 1938, pp38-9.

part of those attending the meeting. If 'Bloody Sunday' was a riot, it was a police riot — a moment of vicious resistance to democratic discussion on the part of the state authorities which could quite easily be compared with the earlier violent repression at Peterloo.

In the summer of 1887 considerable numbers of the increasing ranks of the London unemployed gathered in Trafalgar Square. Many of them were homeless, and the Square provided a place to sleep; the situation is well-depicted in Harkness' contemporary novel, *Out Of Work*.[16] During the summer nights discussion meetings were organised to occupy the unemployed vagrants. The first to address these was the Reverend Thomas Jackson, whose 3.30am open-air lectures would be followed by the provision of meagre breakfasts for his hungry listeners. Before long the socialists began attending the Square to preach their message to the unemployed; the most active and influential orator amongst these was John Burns. On 14 October a meeting was organised in Trafalgar Square to protest against the planned state murders of the framed Chicago anarchists. The speakers included William Morris, Annie Besant, George Bernard Shaw and, from America, Henry George, the author of the immensely popular radical book, *Progress and Poverty*. Socialist meetings in the Square tended to begin in the early afternoon, and were followed by processions of the unemployed into various parts of London. This pattern of popular discussion and demonstration was a cause of some alarm to local business people, who had experienced the Pall Mall riots only a year earlier, and to the state, which was aware that this radical activity was taking place no more than a stone's throw away from parliament in one direction and Buckingham Palace in the other. On 17 October the Metropolitan Police Commissioner, Sir Charles Warren, issued a temporary ban on meetings in Trafalgar Square. Within a fortnight this was overturned by the government's Law Officers, who could see no legal justification for such a ban.

Warren responded by ordering his officers to arrest all speakers whose language was deemed by them to be threatening. Within days three socialist speakers were arrested (Allman, Lynch and George), and attempts to run some meetings were prevented by the force of the police. Warren's immediate fear seems to have been that the unemployed, stirred up by the socialists, would upset the pomp and ceremony being prepared for the Lord Mayor's Day on 9 November. He even went as far as to issue a second ban, in contravention of the Law Officers' ruling, on 31 October. It

16. See Chapter 4.

stated that 'no public meetings will be allowed to assemble in Trafalgar Square, nor will speeches be allowed to be delivered therein'. A predictably British solution quelled the state's fears about an uprising on Lord Mayor's Day: it rained, and most of the revolutionaries very wisely stayed at home or under cover.

A number of socialists did respond to the police ban, and the Law and Liberty League was formed to defend free speech. The Metropolitan Radical Association, which was a collection of socialist, democratic and Irish nationalist organisations in London, called a mass meeting for Sunday, 13 November in defiance of the ban. The meeting had several purposes: to protest against mass unemployment, to express outrage at the legal persecution of the Parnellite Irish journalist, William O'Brien, and to protect the freedom to meet and discuss in public.

The state's response to this attempt to hold a meeting in Trafalgar Square was staggering. Thousands of police were summoned to defend the Square against intrusion by those marching to it from several meeting points in London. No less than 1500 officers cordoned off the Square by forming a human wall, a further 3000 were placed at Nelson's Column, 2500 more were stationed in readiness at Charing Cross, 100 armed cavalry officers were in attendance, and hundreds more were placed strategically along the routes to the Square. As if this excessive force were not enough, a regiment of 200 Life Guards was stationed in Whitehall, and a battalion of Grenadier Guards was close by. It is quite clear that both Warren and the Home Secretary, Henry Matthews, were in readiness for something approaching civil war. Between 20 000 and 50 000 marchers left from various meeting points to make their way to the Square. The overwhelming majority of them set out with no intention to become involved in violence of any kind. The planned speakers at the meeting included Morris, Burns and the Radical MP, Cunninghame Graham; none of these had reason to provoke violence. The police attacked the marchers *en route*, and this led to a raising of the temperature and some violence. One police officer was stabbed in the course of this confrontation by one George Harrison, who was subsequently sentenced to five years imprisonment.

Those who arrived at the Square attempted to break through the police cordon. In his report of the event, entitled 'London in a State of Siege', William Morris described what then happened:

'Once in the Square we were... helpless units... Undoubtedly if 200 or 300 men could have been got to make a rush on the cordon of the police, especially at the south-east corner, the crowd could have swarmed into the Square... But the result would probably have been a far bloodier massacre than Peterloo; for the people, once in the Square, would have found themselves in a mere penfold at the mercy of the police and soldiers. It is true that as matters went, there seemed very little need for the appearance of the latter, so completely were the police, horse and foot, masters of the situation... So that I was fairly surprised, the crowd being then quite quiet, to see the Life Guards form at the north of the Square and march up towards St Martin's Church with the magistrate at their head (a sort of country-gentleman-looking imbecile) to read the Riot Act... A little after this a regiment of the foot-guards made their appearance with fixed bayonets, and completed the triumph of law and order.'[17]

The Square was cleared by early evening. Two hundred people were put in hospital by the day's events, and two of them, Curner and Connell, died as a result of injuries sustained. They had merely been attempting to hold a public meeting. The following week another meeting was called, but Warren extended the ban to include the streets surrounding the Square. Ironically, the meeting was forced to shift to Speakers' Corner where it would be tolerated; in the battle for the right to hold meetings in Hyde Park 20 years' earlier speakers were diverted to Trafalgar Square in order to keep Hyde Park free from the crowd.

On 28 November the socialists attempted one further public meeting in the Square, and in the ensuing battle with the police Alfred Linnell was killed. It was for Linnell's funeral that Morris wrote his stirring 'Death Song'. The occasion attracted tens of thousands of people for whom the murder of Linnell became symbolic of a far broader assault upon free public discussion. Not until 1892 was the state ban upon meetings in Trafalgar Square lifted, and even then it was declared that no meetings may take place without the written permission of the police. This restriction remains to this day. By the time that the Trafalgar Square ban was lifted, open-air speaking had become a regular means of public communication, not only at established sites or in London, but on street corners and in parks throughout the country.

Tommy Jackson joined the SDF in the mid-1890s, and he describes in his autobiography how open-air meetings were held on Sundays 'at some customary "spouting-place"', in order to gather supporters for its evening indoor meetings.[18] The appointment of speakers was a matter of course,

17. Cited in Salmon, op cit, pp302-6.
18. TA Jackson, *Solo Trumpet*, London, 1953, p54.

with usually one person establishing himself as 'a local favourite'. Jackson's suggestion that chairmen were often appointed on the basis of their ability 'to silence rowdy interrupters by laying-out one or two per meeting' can be taken with a pinch of salt. Jackson's fondest early exposure to the outdoor platform was in Finsbury Park, where he would listen to speeches by Con Lehane, an ex-Fenian and now a socialist. (He was to become the first General Secretary of the Socialist Party of Great Britain.) Jackson wrote: 'These Sunday morning meetings were often the peak-point of socialist activity in those years. The proletarians would be virtually turned out of their homes while the Sunday dinner was being prepared; and as the pubs didn't open till 1pm, they would be glad of anything to help pass the time.' It was at one of these meetings in Finsbury Park that Jackson first took the chair for Lehane's meeting, and began his career as 'an agitator and propagandist of some notoriety'. Speaking first for the SDF, then the SPGB, Jackson moved on to become a paid speaker for the Independent Labour Party and, finally, the Communist Party. The phenomenon of the freelance orator is one which we shall meet again in the case of Bonar Thompson, but, according to Jackson's memoirs, he managed to earn an average labourer's wage from collections taken at meetings which he addressed. Jackson's finest open-air oration, in his opinion, was in 1913 in Leeds: a speech on Home Rule made to coincide with a visit to the city by Sir Edward Carson. The condition of the meeting site in Leeds is of some interest:

'Our speaking in Leeds was done occasionally upon Woodhouse Moor, but more usually in the square in front of the Town Hall. Three statues (of Sir Robert Peel, Queen Victoria and the Duke of Wellington) in a line parallel to the front of the Town Hall were by established custom used — or their plinths were — as "pulpits" for outdoor speakers. The centre one (Queen Victoria) to which I established a sort of squatter's right, was the best if one had the voice and the technique to hold a large audience. It was admirable to speak from since the audience could stand, not only in front of the statue on the ground level, but behind it, tier above tier all the way up the Town Hall steps to the broad portico behind the classic pillars. If the speaker's voice was pitched correctly this portico with its roof made a perfect sounding-board.[19]

The bizarre spectacle of a left wing speaker advocating Irish republican-

19. Ibid, pp99-100.

ism using a statue of Queen Victoria as his platform is odd enough, but the thought of a crowd gathered in a fashion not dissimilar to that which would have listened to the orations of Demosthenes before the Athenian assembly is a part of Yorkshire history which should not be forgotten.

Another early member of the Communist Party, Harry Pollitt, who was to become its General Secretary, began his speaking career chairing meetings of the Openshaw Socialist Society outside the Gransmoor Hotel, a pub on the Ashton Old Road, Manchester. Pollitt's first attempt ended with him being lost for words (unlike Jackson, who records that his first attempt at chairing a meeting resulted in him taking over from the speaker). Pollitt was advised by the veteran outdoor orator, Bill Gee, to bear in mind three golden rules: 'Start on time, boost the literature, finish before the pubs close, the workers like time for a drink.'[20] An important institution in Manchester was the County Forum, established in 1812, and still used in the 1930s as a non-partisan meeting place for speakers to train, debate and continue meetings when it rained. A key figure at the Forum was Moses Baritz, an orthodox Marxist as well as being a music critic for *The Manchester Guardian* and an orator whose eccentricity was only exceeded by his passion. One lecture series at the Forum by Baritz was entitled 'The Materialist Interpretation of Literature, Ethics, Art, Drama, Music, History, Politics, the British Constitution, Transport, Morals, Science, Philosophy and the lives of Marx, Engels, Lafargue and Lewis H Morgan'. Such was the autodidactic spirit of the time. An anecdote of Jackson's sums up Baritz's enthusiasm: being physically excluded from a meeting of the Salford British Socialist Party which was to be addressed by their leader, HM Hyndman, Baritz climbed on to the ventilating shaft directly above the platform, 'and provided an obligato-accompaniment to the oratory' of Hyndman by playing his clarinet. He was soon offered a front-row seat at the meeting from which he proceeded to put his questions.[21]

Glasgow also had a meeting place to which all of the outdoor speakers could go for uninterrupted sheltered discussion. Bob Russell, who frequented the Workers Open Forum in Renfrew Street, describes it as 'a forum where workers of all political persuasions could debate their respective political ideas and policies... The WOF committee drew up a programme and invited all the organisations which frequented their hall to send representatives to lecture on their own policies.'[22] The organisations

20. J Mahon, *Harry Pollitt*, London, 1976, p28.
21. Jackson, op cit, p85.
22. Personal correspondence from Bobby Russell, 19 August 1993.

which took advantage of this were the Independent Labour Party, the Revolutionary Communist Party, the SPGB, the Socialist Labour Party, the Industrial Workers of the World, the Communist Party, the Anarchist Federation and, on a few occasions, the Labour Party. In addition to the lectures and discussions, they also organised debates between the various rival organisations. Manny Shinwell describes in his memoirs how his first public debate was organised by the Forum, though it took place in the open air in the adjoining Bird Market before an unseated crowd of over 500.[23] During the winter, when there were less opportunities for street meetings, they organised mid-week evening lectures on Industrial History and Economics. The hall itself was situated above a furniture shop in Renfrew Street; there was seating for several hundred people 'on benches of the type seen in Victorian mission halls'. At the front of the hall was a raised platform from which the speakers gave their addresses. The WOF was an integral feature of the age of popular discussion in Edwardian Glasgow; it survived into the 1950s.[24]

The radical organisations fought for respect in Glasgow mainly by competing for audiences at outdoor meetings. On the eve of the First World War, John Maclean was addressing huge anti-war meetings in Bath Street. The scene was described by MacDougall, a fellow speaker of Maclean's on the British Socialist Party platform:

'It was packed from side to side so that a child could have walked on the heads of the people, and that condition extended a long distance down the street. Week after week there was to be seen a vast body of men and women, standing in tense silence, their attention riveted on the speakers for two or three hours on end... All who attended remember it to this day as one of the most significant experiences of their lives. How can one describe the scene? At the foot of the street across on the opposite side of Renfield Street stood the Tramway Office, brilliantly lit, plastered with poster appeals to men to join the army. Up the street, standing on a table in the midst of a dense crowd... stood John Maclean exhorting men in explicit terms under no circumstances to join the army.'[25]

In 1916 the government's Defence of the Realm Act banned speakers from making statements in opposition to the war, declaring such a democratic liberty to be a criminal offence.

23. M Shinwell, *Lead With The Left: My First Ninety Years*, London, 1982, p94.
24. Russell, op cit.
25. N Milton, *John Maclean*, London, 1973, p82.

In his autobiography, *No Mean Fighter*, Harry McShane, the Glaswegian socialist, recalled Sunday meetings at Glasgow Green where crowds of 300 or 400 people listened to speakers whose platforms stretched as far as Nelson's Monument. They would begin at midday and continue until almost 10 o'clock at night. Interestingly, many of the meetings were on religious topics, sometimes of a quite abstruse theological nature. These differed from Salvation Army street meetings and other evangelistic gatherings, which, whilst sharing the terrain of the outdoor platforms, were essentially rehearsed and non-interactive events.

At the old Glasgow Bird Market, near the Green, seats were put out on Sundays and a platform was erected so that rival speakers could debate against one another. As McShane recalls:

'The thing that made Glasgow Green different from Hyde Park and other open-air speakers' places was that the speakers could challenge one another to debates... The popular time for speakers to challenge each other was on Sunday afternoon at two o'clock; all the lecturers would be speaking, and suddenly there would be a challenge from one to another.'

Debates between Protestants and atheists, Catholics and Protestants, and Irish republicans and Orangemen were recalled by Harry McShane, but, despite the intensity of the intellectual antagonisms, McShane noted the orderliness and educational atmosphere of the meetings: 'We didn't mock the speakers, we only asked questions and we learnt a lot.'[26]

London meetings were the most numerous. After Speakers' Corner in Hyde Park, the most important London speaking place was undoubtedly the so-called Forum east of the Victoria Fountain in Victoria Park, Hackney. (It was known locally as the 'Forum and Agin'em'.) As early as 1842, when the original park site of Bonner's Fields was acquired by the Crown, it was used by rival Christian and free-thought speakers; it was there that the 15-year-old Charles Bradlaugh listened to the oratory of Richard Carlile, the English publisher of Paine's *The Rights of Man*, and was won to atheism. As with Hyde Park, attempts were made to prevent outdoor meetings in Victoria Park, but the ensuing battle for free speech was less dramatic. In 1862 public meetings were forbidden in the park unless prior permission had been granted in writing; this led to a flood of applications, and an eventual decision to open the park to all lawfully-held meetings. Perhaps it was thought by the authorities that working class

26. H McShane and J Smith, *No Mean Fighter*, London, 1978, pp12-14.

discussion in the East End would cause less damage than in Hyde Park, the latter being in the vicinity of expensive West End properties. It can be estimated on the basis of published speakers' lists in various journals that between 1885 and 1939 there were approximately 100 street corner and park meetings per week throughout London. The largest number of plat-forms assembled at Hyde Park, Victoria Park, Finsbury Park and Battersea Common. Harry Wicks, the militant Battersea trade unionist, recalled two of the speakers who were local favourites: Johnny Holmes and Tom Waller, known locally as 'Workhouse Waller' on account of his role in the occupation of the Swaffield Road workhouse in July 1921 to protest against the policy of withholding Poor Relief to the unemployed unless they performed task work. Holmes was remembered by Wicks for his well-delivered attacks upon members of the aristocracy, such as the coal mine owner, the Duke of Northumberland:

'Thirty bob a minute was his income, as much as a miner received for three days work at the coalface. He had an infectious smile, as though he was laughing at his own speech. "Imagine, 30 shillings each minute of the day. Whatever the Duke was doing, going to bed, eating his bread and cheese or sitting in the bathroom having a sh-sh-sh-shave." Each itemisa-tion of the crowded minutes in the Duke's life brought fresh convulsions of laughter from the crowd.'[27]

In his memoirs, Ralph Fox recalled how he first stumbled upon the open-air platform in West Green Road, Tottenham whilst out with a friend searching for female companionship. Leaving his friend to secure a liai-son with a girl, Fox wandered in the direction of a Salvation Army band which, having completed its night's work, made way to its citadel 'with bonneted girls shaking their tambourines'. Their departure 'left the ground free for orators, agitators, world-shakers and evangelists of various kinds', recalled Fox.[28]

Upon encountering the Edinburgh-born socialist, Alex Anderson, Fox

27. H Wicks, *Keeping My Head: Memoirs of a British Bolshevik*, London, 1992, pp20-1.
28. Douglas Hyde recalled the wide range of debate that occurred on the Downs, an open grassy hill in Bristol, in the 1920s: 'On the Downs almost any night you could find orators representing the Conservative, Liberal, Labour and Communist Parties; "high" Anglicans, low churchmen, respectable Nonconformists who worship in chapels, and the less respectable ones who carry boards proclaiming that God is not mocked and who sing revivalist hymns to the accompaniment of wheezy portable harmoniums... On the Downs spiritual and intellectual battles were fought.' (D Hyde, *I Believed*, London, 1952, p7)

was captivated by the oratory. Rarely has the power of the open-air platform so forcefully been portrayed:

'In the moonlight the speaker's head and shoulders were silhouetted clearly above the crowd. Round him the audience was gathered, a solid mass of white, attentive faces. He had reached that point — known to every artist in words — when the audience and himself had fallen under the spell. In loud clear tones he was voicing the gospel of discontent. I stood and listened. Here was a man appealing to that youthful blood which, in every generation, is ready to pour itself out in sacrifice to cleanse the world... He rose to his climax and, unconsciously, the audience leaned forward...'[29]

Anderson called upon his listeners to join him in crossing the Rubicon; they applauded before dispersing reluctantly, and young Ralph Fox knew that his 'life would never be the same again'. Convinced that 'if established society could have fallen before oratory... Anderson would have brought it down', he made a point of listening to him whenever he could. Anderson was a remarkably energetic speaker; listings in *The Socialist Standard* indicate that he addressed three outdoor meetings each Sunday, as well as weekday ones. (He was to die prematurely at the age of 47, largely as a result of exhaustion and poverty.) What was the appeal of this speaker to a young man like Fox?

'I could not resist these avalanches of oratory, especially as Anderson gave expression to all those feelings of resentment and bitterness which I could not put into words. My only regret was that I had to be up so early in the morning that I could not stay to the end of these long-distance speeches, except when on some specially interesting occasion I abandoned all thought of the morrow... It was hard... having to spend the long black week waiting for Sunday, to be caught up and carried away in these denunciations and appeals.'[30]

On one level this seems to endorse the Le Bonist thesis: what role did Anderson perform for Fox and the many others who heard him which amounted to more than a simplistic imagery of discontent, and a futile Sunday escapism from the realities of existence? The conservative reading of what was happening is tempting, but facile. Much more was going on

29. Fox, op cit, p33.
30. Ibid, p37.

at these outdoor meetings than remote analysis can perceive. The role of the orator as one who puts into words, and indeed logical connection, disgruntled thoughts and fragmented visions was not a process whereby the speaker's eloquence displaced the independent thinking of the listeners, but one whereby the collective ability to reason on the basis of experience was enhanced. Here were crowds whose only real participation in any kind of a democratic culture, apart from trade union involvement in the cases of a minority of them, was in the anonymity of the polling booth. The open-air meeting socialised the activity of deciding who should rule and what policies should be pursued. There can be no serious debate on specific issues until general principles have been considered, and this is why so many of the outdoor orators spoke of vast visions and sweeping theoretical insights. In what other forum could the crowd be exposed to real choice as to first principles? Far from being an exercise in escapism, the delight in the performance of the orators often gave rise to a practical decision to enter into political commitments, often becoming more energy-consuming than the conventional labours of the working week. Fox himself joined Anderson's party, and subsequently became a speaker himself. Indeed, all of the people whose observations as listeners to the outdoor platform we have considered in this chapter went on to become speakers themselves. The assertion of the 'mass psychologists' that these events encouraged passivity or submission to platform leadership is empirically simply untrue; indeed, it is hard to think of any other medium of communication where the interchangeability of speaker and auditor has been easier or more frequent.

None of this has prevented a succession of superficialities from being committed to paper in scores of newspaper and magazine articles on the open-air platform over the decades, each vying with one another to search for the more disparaging clichés to reflect the eccentricity and indignity of such discourse. A good example, notable for its unimaginative typicality rather than literary merit, appears in VS Pritchett's *London Perceived*, in which Speakers' Corner is compared to 'a dog show' where the speakers appear to be barking about subjects 'often trivial or farcical'. The standards of debate, Pritchett informs his readers, 'are low and primitive', although to what he is comparing them we are not told — the House of Commons, or the Lords; the Oxford Union, or five-minute confrontations between politicians on the television? The vastly different environments for such discussion must be taken into account. How many Prime Ministers have had to answer parliamentary questions in the middle of a rain storm? How many speakers at the Oxford Union have had to carry their own platform to the debate on two buses and along a crowded shopping street? How often are the TV debaters allowed to settle themselves in a lounge before entering combat, and how many of them would be prepared to carry their convictions to their audiences by speaking for hours, often against the noise of unhelpful disrupters, rather than for a few minutes within a secure studio? But with disregard for the unique openness of uncontrolled interactive discussion, Pritchett proceeds condescendingly to sneer at the folly of these barking democrats:

'Some old gent — I've seen him for years — dribbles on about there being millions of gallons of water up in the sky... There are the Irish, storming away about the men in gaol in Belfast. There are the Communists, arguing with the young. There are men who want the West Indians out, and those who want them in. A lonely figure disputes the Virgin birth; an elderly men tells us the pyramids hold the key to human destiny.'[31]

JH Rooney, writing about Victoria Park in *Harpers Magazine* in February 1888, showed less contempt as he saw scattered before him 'numerous groups, some of them very closely packed. Almost all the religious sects of England and all the political and social parties are preaching their ideas and disputing...' For Rooney, writing nearly three-quarters of a century before Pritchett, was less confident about the possibility of marginalising the Age of Discussion. Late Victorian and Edwardian writers had no choice but to take seriously the open-air political meeting; theirs was an age when even the Conservative Party had need of the platforms of the Primrose League and the Anti-Socialist Union to counter what they saw as the pernicious influence of the socialist and anarchist orators; religious preachers had come to recognise that the parks contained more souls in need of them than the pews; even the statesmen, for so long secluded in self-contained institutions of government, began to venture into the streets to compete for support. (By the 1890s the open-air platform was becoming a key feature of electoral activity.) It seemed then that the right to dissent and persuade in public places was a defining quality of the finest kind of liberal democracy. Stanley Fish, in the boyishly provocative title essay of his book, *There's No Such Thing as Free Speech, and It's a Good Thing, Too,* is peculiarly dismissive of the reality of existing public discussion, asserting:

31. VS Pritchett, *London Perceived*, London, 1986, pp49-50.

'... freedom of expression would only be a primary value if it didn't matter what was said, didn't matter in the sense that no one gave a damn but just liked to hear talk. There are contexts like that, a Hyde Park corner or a call-in talk show where people get to sound off for the sheer fun of it. These, however, are special contexts, artificially bounded spaces designed to assure that talking is not taken seriously.'[32]

Apart from its offensive condescension, such analysis betrays a sad lack of historical knowledge of the power which such talk can have, especially when one considers that several chapters of Professor Fish's book consist of a rather precious debate between two liberal arts academics about the appropriate and inappropriate use of language in American universities.

Early British newsreels exhibited the open-air platform as evidence of a flourishing civic culture. Nobody believed that the talk was an exercise in fun or eccentric political irrelevance. It was a kind of democratic freedom which discomforted those unused to it, as Antonio Gramsci noted in one of his prison letters of 1918:

'An Italian university professor told me about something that happened to him in Hyde Park, London, and as he spoke he was still trembling with noble indignation. He saw some citizens plant a banner in the ground, climb up on a chair, attract the attention of some passers-by, and begin to give a lecture. He saw about 20 of them doing this, each putting forward his own ideas and trying to make converts. Some were followers of particular Protestant sects, others were socialists, anarchists and theologists. He stopped in front of an anarchist, and was so outraged by the things he heard that he immediately turned to a nearby policeman and, appalled as he was, asked him: "What on earth are you standing there for, why don't you shut this character up?" The policeman replied calmly: "The reason I'm here is to shut up people like you who would like to stop others having freedom of speech." An English policeman giving a lesson in liberalism to an Italian university professor!'[33]

32. S Fish, *There's No Such Thing as Free Speech, and It's a Good Thing, Too*, Oxford, 1994, pp106-7.
33. A Gramsci, *Scritti giovanili, 1914-18*, Turin, 1958, p172, kindly translated for me by Howard Moss of University College, Swansea.

Agricultural workers' meeting at the Eleanor Cross,
Geddington, Northamptonshire
[*The Graphic*, 30 November 1872]

Louis-Adolphe Gautier, *Stump Speaking*

Bonar Thompson, the famous Hyde Park orator

The cover of Bonar Thompson's autobiography, *Hyde Park Orator*

A lifetime of oratory: Donald Soper, 1994
[Photograph: Philip Wolmuth]

Anyone for debate?
[Photograph: Philip Wolmuth]

The unfortunate public image of Speakers' Corner
[Photograph: Philip Wolmuth]

A dying tradition? Public orators and attentive listeners at
Speakers' Corner
[Photograph: Nick White]

The one-way discussion, Speakers' Corner, 1993
[Photograph: Philip Wolmuth]

The limits of free speech: comedian Tony Allen is arrested
at Speakers' Corner in 1979 after criticising the Queen
[Photograph: Philip Wolmuth]

No right of public access, Sicilian Avenue, Holborn, London

Meetings of the Imagination

ON 27 November 1909 the Hackney and Shoreditch edition of the Marxist journal *Justice* published a poem by Rose E Sharland which celebrated the efforts of 'The Street Corner Orator':

Aloft on his stool o'er the crowd,
Prophetic and earnest he stands.
His bearing defiant, unbowed
By toil that has coarsened his hands.
His face, weather-beaten and worn,
Stray silver amid the black hair,
Deep eyes that behold a new morn
Arising o'er hills of despair.
A spirit wide-soaring and strong,
That thrills through each eloquent word,
Magnetic it flows, till the throng
To swifter emotion is stirred.
His gestures are free as his tongue,
He throws down the gauntlet to power,
Imaginary monsters are flung
To earth, where 'neath clenched hands they cower.
Behind him a dark silhouette
The factory giants arise,
Where daily men toil and forget
The wonder of woodland and skies.
But now, looking up, they behold
The glory of cloud-gleam and star;
His words a new era unfold,
And Hope seems nor laggard nor far,
He speaks of a day when the earth
Shall give all her bounty to all,
With labour a blessing, and mirth
To dance where the shadows now fall.
A herald of Hope for a space,

To-morrow to labour he goes.
But, lighting his fine furrowed face
Is joy of the Truth that he knows.

This is the uncomplicated image of the orator as the bringer of truth. The speaker's oratory radiates the light of hope; the listeners thrill to the sound of his eloquent prophecies of the future that could be theirs. From Wesleyan field meetings to street corner socialists, all that had changed was the geography of vision: for the Christian preachers hope fertilised the rural soil; for the socialists the narrow urban streets were the ground upon which widened horizons were mapped; the Methodists' world to come was celestial in location; the socialists sited utopia upon the earthly ruins of decaying industrial capitalism. The function of both rhetorical appeals was similar: the aspiration to become fully human, driven by that most uniquely human possession, the power of speech.

The readers of *Justice* were accustomed to the open-air platform; it was as normal to their discourse as were the dingy pub rooms and coffee houses in which self-education was conducted within an atmosphere of autodidactic striving for clarity of class expression. These were members of a class which had been excluded from the expectation of articulate debate. Physically excluded from the institutions of learning and respectable discourse, and economically confined to think for themselves only in the unexploited spare hours of darkness and on days off which were appropriated culturally as the Lord's Day, the poor had reason to regard self-expression as being in itself a revolutionary act: an intrusion into a forbidden zone. So it was that to the minority of workers who read radical literature such as *Justice* (as well as the other radical publications of late Victorian and Edwardian Britain), the exercise of rhetorical propaganda was not merely a means to an end, but a moment of cultural arrival, a practical reclamation of the workers' minds and voices from the abyss of the ruling ideology.

Part of the ideological rupture which open-air oratory represented concerned the very form of working class speech. In England, perhaps more than anywhere else, the relationship between accent and power has been central. Shaw's *Pygmalion* could not have had such a political resonance in any other nation state. The dominant view was that those who could not speak 'properly' were unlikely to have much worth saying. As menials, the inarticulate were expected to do their best to be understood by those above them, primarily by speaking in questions and with a humble obsequiousness. ('Is Sir ready for his dinner?' would seem to reflect the anticipated heights of working class speech.) Amongst themselves the working class was perceived as speaking a form of English of intrinsically low value. The inferiority of form left no doubt as to the insignificance of content. As PJ Keating has pointed out, cockney London speech was regarded by British writers of the last century as not just another distinctive regional dialect, but as indicating 'automatically' an 'inferior social status' — 'the language of the slums'.[1] In taking this slum language (not just cockney, but the many accents of the poor) and using it within the social environment of the slums to expound messages of professed wisdom, the open-air orators presented a profound cultural challenge to the preconceptions of outside observers, particularly the literary elite who saw it as their business to represent life as it was, but all too often found such representation distorted by class prejudice.

The most obvious — and disruptive — problem faced by professional writers of both fiction and non-fiction came when strikes had to be described. It was this subject which so seriously flawed Dickens' otherwise masterly critique of capitalist utilitarianism in *Hard Times*. Written shortly after the author had returned from a journalistic expedition to Preston, where he was inescapably faced with the clear antagonisms of the class struggle of his age in the fiercely contested strike of the Lancashire textile workers, his novel assaults the callous ethos of the industrial exploiters with a ruthless accuracy, and then flinches and flees from any expression of sympathy in depicting the strikers and their militant defence of class interests. Interestingly, it is by estranging his readers from the language of the strikers that Dickens succeeds in distancing support from those whom the logic of his novel would lead us to support. And it is relevant that the description of a strikers' meeting (held not outdoors, but in a 'densely crowded and suffocatingly close hall') is used as the setting for Dickens' attack upon the vociferous poor.

The orator, a trade union organiser called Slackbridge, does not simply speak, but roars at the top of his voice, emitting 'froth and fume'. The passion in his oratory was in no way the result of the justice of his words, but was, Dickens tells his readers, a substitute for the 'safe solid sense' of his working class listeners. For we are told that the orator, far from having more worth hearing than those listening to him, has less right to be heard because compared with the men in the crowd he 'was not so honest... not so manly... not so good-humoured... [and] was essentially below them'. It surprises Dickens to see such submission on the part of the

1. PJ Keating, *The Working Classes In Victorian Fiction*, London, 1971, pp247-8.

many to a speaker of such complacent inanities. Before the second account of the orator's words, Dickens prepares his readers' prejudices with this description: 'The orator having refreshed himself, wiped his corrugated forehead from left to right several times with his handkerchief folded into a pad, and concentrated all his revived forces in a sneer of great disdain and bitterness.' Thus introduced, Slackbridge's commencing words, 'But, oh my friends and brothers! Oh men and Englishmen, the downtrodden operatives of Coketown!', is established as insincere — the hypocrisy of a mob manipulator. Again, responding to Stephen Blackpool's defence of treachery against the union: 'Slackbridge jumped up and stood beside him, gnashing and tearing.'[2] Such bias of language set a precedent for numerous reports of strike meetings in the twentieth-century press.

As far as Dickens was concerned, there was no duty to reflect any humanity in the character of a trade union orator, with his 'habitually sour expression'. As for the crowd, its role was confined to the cheering and hissing of the Roman Circus; it is, in fact, a classical Le Bonist assembly of the easily impressionable. It distresses Dickens 'to see this crowd of earnest faces, whose honesty in the main no competent observer free from bias could doubt, so agitated by such a leader'. But Dickens was not that 'competent observer free from bias'. His prejudice against the oratorical pretensions and manipulative powers of radicals was clear as early as 1836 in his *Sketches by Boz*. It is in those short accounts of London life that readers are introduced to 'The Parlour Orator', a character called Rogers who represented a type to be found, according to Dickens, in every 'parlour, or club-room, or benefit society, or humble party of any kind'. Such orators are invariably 'weak-pated dolts' who do 'a great deal of mischief... to their cause'. What is it that Dickens so disliked about such orators? Their readiness to employ rhetoric to impress the gullible seems to have been their chief crime. And indeed, Rogers' use of high-sounding words as proof to his greengrocer adversary that the latter is really 'a willing slave' does seem to be too easy a victory in argument. But most pub debates were not — and are not — settled in this fashion; Rogers, the red-faced, cigar-puffing know-all, is a caricature of Dickens' creation, but there is no evidence that popular debate in nineteenth-century London was ever influenced by people like him. Dickens seems to be objecting to the fact that men frequent pubs in order to debate matters of political and philosophical significance, and that some of them have a

2.   C Dickens, *Hard Times*, Harmondsworth, 1987, pp169-76.

command of language which impresses or affects others. Such disdain or irritation is an expression of class prejudice, disguised as humour, as in the following caricatured image of the pub speaker:

'"What is a man?", continued the red-faced specimen of the species, jerking his hat indignantly from its peg on the wall. "What is an Englishman? Is he to be trampled upon by every oppressor? Is he to be knocked down at everybody's bidding? What's freedom? Not a standing army. What's a standing army? Not freedom? What's general happiness? Not universal misery. Liberty ain't the window tax, is it? The Lords ain't the Commons, are they?" And the red-faced man, gradually bursting into a radiating sentence, in which such adjectives as "dastardly", "oppressive", "violent" and "sanguinary" formed the most conspicuous words, knocked his hat indignantly over his eyes, left the room, and slammed the door after him.
  '"Wonderful man!", said he of the sharp nose.
  '"Splendid speaker!", added the broker.
  '"Great power!", said everybody but the greengrocer.'[3]

This is an amusing anecdotal sketch, to be sure, but in reality who would ever be so aroused by the disjointed and illogical ramblings of a pub oracle? When transferred from the harmless pseudo-moot of the pub parlour to the industrial class struggle, the easily bemused vulnerability of the listeners and the vicious intent of the orator is transformed from comic observation to bitterness.

  In *Hard Times* oratory gives rise to mass anger which commences with the ostracism of Stephen Blackpool, and culminates in his death. This line of consequence was followed by other Victorian novelists who saw in working class oratory murderous outcomes. For example, in George Eliot's *Felix Holt, The Radical* the power of open-air oratory is sensed as an ominous threat, and it culminates in riot and manslaughter. The threat is indicated from the outset. Readers are introduced to Harold Transome, the respectable politician, as 'one of those people... to whose presence in the room you could not be indifferent: if you do not hate or dread them, you must find the touch of their hands, nay, their very shadows, agreeable.' Holt, by contrast, is described as 'a man with a troublesome tongue'. Transome's initial view of 'the radical', Holt, is that he is the sort of 'formidable fellow' who is 'capable of mounting a cart in the market-

3. C Dickens, *Sketches by Boz*, London, nd, pp175-6.

place tomorrow and cross-examining me, if I say anything that doesn't please him'. In short, the kind of person politicians would prefer to live without.

Felix Holt is presented as an idealist: 'I'm determined never to go about making my face simpering or solemn, and telling professional lies for profit; or to get tangled in affairs where I must wink at dishonesty and pocket the proceeds, and justify that knavery as part of a system that I can't alter.' To this end Holt commits himself to a radical style of honest oratory: 'I want to be a demagogue of a new sort; an honest one, if possible, who will tell the people they are blind and foolish, and neither flatter them nor fatten on them.'

But when Holt's high-principled working class approach to open-air speaking is put to the test in the course of the North Loamshire electoral contest, the consequence is disorder and disaster. On nomination day, Holt wanders towards the Fox and Hounds inn, 'the ultra-Liberal quarter of the High Street', where he is attracted by a street orator 'whose bare arms were powerfully muscular', and whose 'voice was high and not strong', but reflected 'the fluency and the method of a habitual preacher or lecturer'. The speaker's fine speech in favour of votes for workers inspires Felix to follow him on to the stone upon which he had stood, and his listeners were 'unconsciously influenced' by the grandeur of his voice and stature. This disjunction between the crowd and conscious reflection is crucial to the literary description.

As the election proceeds, the unconscious nature of the crowd becomes apparent even to Felix Holt, who observes that it is composed of 'poor noisy simpletons'. 'The shouting and roaring of rude men is so hideous', bleats his genteel companion, Esther. Before long 'the majority of the crowd were excited with drink', and Felix is left to witness 'the blind outrages of this mad crowd'. He intervenes with a view to taming the mob, but his address to the crowd ends in misunderstanding and violence. As Eliot informs her readers: 'A man with a definite will and an energetic personality acts as a sort of flag to draw and bind together the foolish units of a mob.' The connection is made: the idealistic and articulate 'demagogue of a new sort' falls victim to the blind, drunken, unconscious spite and folly of those to whose intelligence he so naively appealed. This is no mere literary narrative; this is an ideological discourse — a claim about the limitations of mass consciousness. In November 1867 the ideological assumptions were laid bare in the *Address To Working Men*, written by George Eliot and signed in the name of Felix Holt, in which the workers of England were warned against the utopian dangers of organising for full political democracy. Instead they should prepare to accept the lesser evil, and make efforts to improve themselves morally.[4]

A later Victorian anti-democrat, whose early novels provide us with some of the finest depictions of the London working class of his time, was George Gissing. The complexities and paradoxes of Gissing's social outlook, and its reflection of a life of extreme disappointments and simmering class frustration, are best considered in a biographical context. (John Halperin's excellent account of Gissing's life is the best place to start.)[5] Like Dickens, whom he admired enormously and about whom he wrote a literary study, Gissing made no effort to conceal his disdain for working class oratory. In his seventh novel, *The Nether World* (1889), readers are introduced to John Hewett, who 'found much satisfaction in spending his Sunday evenings on Clerkenwell Green, where fervent, if ungrammatical, oratory was to be heard, and participation in debate was open to all whom the spirit moved'. Sidney Kirkwood, the respectable artisan of the novel, and a neighbour of Hewett's, befriends this man whose 'brief, stammering protests against this or that social wrong had such an honest, indeed such a pathetic sound'.[6] Gissing was the first novelist to write about working class life after the custom of open-air street meetings had become established as a regular means of democratic discussion rather than as riotous outbursts. But Gissing's negative depiction of Hewett's Clerkenwell meetings owed more to his antipathy to democracy than to any requirement of his plot. It is hardly coincidental that part of his research for his slum novels took him to the very spot where he places Hewett; as he wrote in a letter: 'Last Sunday evening I spent on Clerkenwell Green – a great assembly-place for radical meetings and the like. A more disheartening scene is difficult to imagine – the vulgar, blatant scoundrels!'[7] This from a writer whose contempt for the intellect of most workers knew no bounds was hardly a surprising observation, but it does help us to see how Kirkwood's neighbour became not merely an attendee of outdoor meetings, but of specifically inarticulate and time-wasting ones.

Three years before writing *The Nether World*, Gissing took it upon himself to dispose of the ethics of socialists and the practicability of so-

4. G Eliot, *Felix Holt, The Radical*, Harmondsworth, 1977, p273, 363, 366, 395-8, 416, 421-2, 607-27.
5. J Halperin, *Gissing: A Life in Books*, Oxford, 1982.
6. G Gissing, *The Nether World*, London, 1986, p53.
7. Halperin, op cit, pp99-100.

71

cialism in his novel *Demos: A Story of English Socialism*. It was written partly in response to the widespread anti-socialist feeling following the Pall Mall riots. In researching it Gissing attended at least one meeting of the Socialist League, and the character of Westlake, the civilising force amongst the novel's socialists, is clearly meant to be William Morris, whose commitment to revolutionary socialist politics baffled and disturbed Gissing. The principal socialist character in *Demos*, Richard Mutimer, is a classic manifestation of Gissing's intense snobbery. He is a bright artisan with a capacity to sway a crowd through oratory: 'His voice was strong and clear; it would ring out well in public places, which is equivalent to saying that it hardly invited too intimate conference.' Gissing found it virtually impossible to praise a working class quality without expressing disgust at the corrupting environment in which it was to be discovered.

Readers are first introduced to Mutimer's oratory at the Islington Commonwealth Hall, the meeting place of Westlake's Socialist Union (based upon Morris' Socialist League). Gissing offers a vivid picture of the Hall – not unlike Russell's description of the Glasgow Workers Open Forum quoted in Chapter Three. Gissing's parodied account of Mutimer's speech on the land question utilises the same devices of ridicule employed by Dickens in his depiction of red-faced Rogers; rhetoric is shown to overwhelm serious substance, and therefore, whatever the merits of Mutimer's message or its undoubted effects upon his hearers, the overall sense is of the irrepressible inferiority of the communicator:

'He spoke of the land; he attacked the old monopoly, and visioned a time when a claim to individual ownerships of the earth's surface would be as ludicrous as were now the assertion of title to a fee-simple somewhere in the moon. He mustered statistics; he adduces historic and contemporary example of the just and the unjust in landholding; he gripped the throat of a certain English duke, and held him up for flagellation; he drifted into oceans of economic theory; he sat down by the waters of Babylon; he climbed Pisgah. Had he but spoken of backslidings in the wilderness!'

As he spoke he began drop his aitches and 'forget his syntactical lapses'. Condescendingly, the snob, Gissing, applauds Mutimer for his honest convictions and a greater ability than most workers to express his views. But still the rhetoric is belittled, the flaws in conventional form noted with just the slightest of sneers, the rhetorical excesses offered for the mirth of his superior readers. And where a mood of patronising restraint pervades the depiction of Mutimer, little is spared when the speeches from the floor by Messrs Cullen and Cowes are reported: 'Mr Cullen rises, at the same time rises Mr Cowes. These two gentlemen are fated to rise simultaneously. They scowl at each other. Mr Cullen begins to speak, and Mr Cowes, after a circular glance of protest, resumes his seat. The echoes tell that we are in for oratory with a vengeance.' In fact, what Gissing's readers are 'in for' are a couple of crude caricatures of self-indulging rhetoricians of the worst kind. Cullen is a man with 'lungs of vast power':

'His vein is King Cambyses'; he tears passion to tatters; he roars leonine; he is your man to have at the pamper's jades of Asia! He has got hold of a new word, and that the verb to "exploit". I am exploited, thou art exploited – he exploits! Who? Why, such men as that English duke whom the lecturer gripped and flagellated. The English duke is Mr Cullen's bugbear; never a speech from Mr Cullen but that duke is most horribly mauled.'

The worker with his newly-discovered words offends Gissing. The alternative, of course, would be for workers to confine their speech with humility to the limited lexicon of their elementary school educations. Mr Cowes is contrasted with Mr Cullen not in quality but style: his tone is 'quietly venomous', and he regards his fellows 'with wrathful intensity'. Rather than these orators (whose insincerity is secured by the author in the final paragraphs of the chapter by placing them together in the same public house after having condemned the evils of drink), Gissing admires the speech from the floor made by the meanest and most pessimistic member of the audience, a wretched figure who warns the workers that all social change would be a waste of time until their class 'first make ourselves worthy of such freedom'. This message – which proves to be the moral thrust of the novel – is conspicuously similar to Felix Holt's *Address to the Working Men.* [8]

For the Victorian novelists, public meetings were imagined in terms of threat. The idealist reformer or the self-educating artisan is depicted as the misused victim of the thoughtless, amorphous mob whose collective viciousness would always overwhelm the higher qualities of the former. However romanticised the expression of sympathy for the deprived, no such empathic warmth characterises the Victorian novelists' approach to

8.   G Gissing, *Demos: A Story of English Socialism*, London, 1886, Chapter 6.

73

the thinking, speaking, collectively discussing working class. The battered bodies and squalid dwelling places of the downtrodden invited abundant sentiments of human warmth, but the active minds and expressive tongues of the poor met with ridicule, contempt and ill-concealed fear. It is precisely this border between seeing and hearing – close enough to peer at poverty, but at a sufficient distance for the voices of the impoverished to be of no significance – which marked the remoteness of the Victorian novelists from the reality of their times, and caused them to subject most working class speech to parody or exclusion. The one Victorian novelist who did reflect the existence of the open-air meetings, which by the last quarter of the century were becoming a feature of urban life, was Margaret Harkness, who wrote under the name of John Law. Although she wrote several novels, she is remembered for the three written in the 1880s which attempted to depict the lives of workers in the East End of London. Harkness wrote these novels – *A City Girl*, *Out of Work* and *Captain Lobe: A Story of the Salvation Army* – during her brief period as a member of the Marxist Social Democratic Federation, and it was doubtlessly the active involvement of this organisation in open-air oratory which led her to include references to it in her writing. Although not a speaker herself, she was very close to HH Champion, a socialist orator of some note. Harkness is the first Victorian novelist to write of outdoor meetings not as a sneering and rather frightened observer from the sidelines, but as one who believed in the power of oratory as a positive political force (albeit rather half-heartedly, as it turned out from her later abandonment of the socialist faith and support for the Salvation Army).

In *Out Of Work*, published in 1888, the open-air meetings in Victoria Park are first encountered through two very different visions: that of Polly Elwin, a Methodist, and her boyfriend, Jos Coney, an unemployed carpenter. Walking romantically through the park one Sunday 'to look at the people, and hear the music' (though Polly has doubts as to the sanctity of the latter activity on the Lord's Day), they encounter a crowd under the trees. At first Polly is pleased to see men preaching. But it soon became clear that the open and critical nature of these discussions were far removed from the rigidity of her Methodist classes. From one platform lectured 'a black man with a flower in his button-hole, and his hat at the back of his head', who sought to explain the evolution of the idea of God (this is undoubtedly a reference to Celestine Edwards, a well-known West Indian speaker for the Christian Evidence Society who was popular in Victoria Park at that time); from another 'shouted a Socialist:

"Don't you know that the men who rule over you are but a handful, and nothing to be afraid of? If you are men, rise up!'"; a Conservative spoke about the price of land, and a freethinker proclaimed that 'God is all a trick of conscience'. Jos is impressed by the speakers, especially the socialist, whom he resolves to visit. Polly is appalled: 'Let's get away from these dreadful people... their talk's downright wicked. Come away, Jos.' This is the dying voice of timorous Victorianism in the face of free speech. Jos ignores it, and in the next chapter goes to visit the speaker he had heard previously on Mile End Waste, near the People's Palace. For the first time a novel allows us a glimpse of the orator within a human dimension beyond the platform. The man, a dock labourer, lives in a squalid dwelling amidst second-hand books, leaflets and old newspapers. It is here that we discover the motive for his speaking: he has a baby, and although he entertains no hope for his own future:

'... the thought of his child made him preach, if happily there might be any good in preaching. Had he been able to take his baby into Victoria Park, to feel its little head in the hollow of his hand when he stood on the Waste, he might perhaps have risen to a pitch of enthusiasm, which would have moved his hearers. Without that stimulus he could only be bitter; and his bitter speeches fell useless."[9]

They go together to the Mile End Waste, where another speaker has commenced the meeting, and here for the only time in a Victorian novel the speaker's appeal is reproduced not to be derided or feared, but as inspiration. Harkness has no great feel for the culture of outdoor meetings beyond a vague political sense of their function, and a romantic sympathy for those for whom these were the only public voice. Better accounts of speakers and speaking were to come, but not until the dawning of the new century.

Owen in *The Ragged Trousered Philanthropists* is in many ways the archetypal soapbox orator. Although he speaks at an outdoor meeting only once in the novel, the entire thrust and style of his arguing is that of the street-corner speaker. Owen's socialist rhetoric is, of course, that of the novel's author, Robert Tressell (whose real name was Robert Noonan), and the interaction between the socialist protagonist and his reactionary workmates presents a microcosmic account of the tense relationship between the Marxist SDF, to which Noonan belonged, and the workers en-

9.   John Law (Margaret Harkness), *Out of Work*, London, 1990, Chapter 3.

countered by its propagandists at their frequently-held open-air meetings. So, although the outdoor platform features only twice in the course of the novel, the many occasions when Owen addresses his fellow workers informally tend to simulate the atmosphere and form of an open-air meeting. The first image of workers gathering in the main street of Mugsborough (Hastings) in *The Ragged Trousered Philanthropists* is reminiscent of the situation in 1886 at Trafalgar Square, where the unemployed gathered, threatening their social superiors through their collective presence:

'... none of them had anything to speak of to do, and the workmen no longer troubled to go to the different shops asking for a job. They knew it was of no use. Most of them just walked about aimlessly *or stood talking in groups in the streets*, principally in the neighbourhood of the Wage Slave Market near the fountain on the Grand Parade. They congregated here in such numbers that one or two residents wrote to the local papers complaining of the "nuisance", and pointing out that it was calculated to drive the "better-class" visitors out of the town. After this two or three extra policemen were put on duty near the fountain with instructions to "move on" any groups of unemployed that formed. They could not stop them from coming there, but they prevented them standing about.' [My emphasis]

Such was the sense of threat attached to congregating, talking workers. The invasion of the town in July by men on bicycles distributing socialist leaflets is clearly based upon the realistic imagery of the Clarionettes, whose early twentieth-century cycling clubs were a unique combination of leisure activity and political propaganda. Their leaflets were advertising an open-air meeting in 'the field at the Cross Roads on the hill at Windley, on Tuesday evening next at 8pm'. Where a tradition of open-air oratory did not exist — which would presumably have been the case in a relative political backwater like Mugsborough/Hastings — it would have been necessary to advertise a meeting in this way. In London and other major cities by the 1900s such advertising was unnecessary; people simply knew that at certain places and times at least somebody would be holding forth.

When Tressell/Noonan comes to describe the meeting, there is a reversal of the previous depictions of the crowds. Hitherto the threatening nature of the mob had been irresponsibly stimulated by cunning or foolish speakers. But the unprecedented socialist intent of this narrative leads to a different account of the Le Bonist irrationality of the crowd. Here the speakers are the bringers of rationality and orderly debate, and the crowd, partly through ignorance and the frustration of boredom, but also as a result of the insidious propaganda fed to them by the anti-socialists, are the brutish disrupters of democratic order. Even before the van from which the meeting is to be addressed arrives, 'it was quite evident that the crowd meant mischief', and when it does arrive it is 'surrounded by a howling mob'. Described as a 'horde of savages', the prejudiced crowd refuse to let the speaker be heard. Instead he is struck on his forehead by a stone by a cheering, shrieking, cursing mob which was 'howling like wolves'. The successful disruption of the meeting culminates in its closure, and then, better still, a new meeting addressed by an anti-socialist. (In the 1900s the Tory-run Anti-Socialist Union was indeed running almost as many meetings as the socialists.) As it turns out, the battle was won that Tuesday night, when the voices of socialists were silenced by violence, but the propaganda war was not over. The socialists make a further attempt to hold an outdoor meeting the following Sunday, and even go to the expense of paying the fare for a speaker to travel down from London by train. This costly effort is in vain, for 'when the socialists came they found the field at the Cross Roads in the possession of a furious, hostile mob, who refused to allow them to speak, and finally they had to go away without having held a meeting'. But they returned, and, as was the case in many places where real attempts were made to establish a regular platform for unorthodox ideas, the right to hold meetings was finally won. But at what price? A speaker injured, almost fatally as we discover – and as we also discover, it is more than a physical wound that he sustained. And socialists, who claimed to be speaking for the benefit of their fellow workers, had to bear the harshest indignity of those workers themselves demanding the right not to be able to hear the case for socialism. Well might some of the socialists have wondered about the value of seeking to make the deaf hear.

It is this sense of betrayal which pervades *The Ragged Trousered Philanthropists*. Perhaps Noonan's motive for literary expression (which was unpublished in his lifetime) was itself compensatory: if the workers would not listen he could at least portray the image and consequences of their non-hearing. Owen feels betrayed by his gullible workmates:

'Usually after one of these arguments, Owen would wander off by himself, with his head throbbing and a feeling of unutterable depression and misery at his heart; weighed down by a growing conviction of the hopelessness of everything, of the folly of expecting that his fellow workmen would ever be willing to try to understand for themselves the causes that produced their sufferings.'

As Noonan observes with sardonic wit:

'Some people deny themselves the necessities or comforts of life in order that they may help to fatten a publican. Others deny themselves in order to enable a lazy parson to live in idleness and luxury; and others spend much time and money that they really need for themselves in buying socialist literature to give away to people who don't want to know about socialism.'

It is this kind of frustration which leads to the particular act of betrayal discovered by Owen's fellow socialist, Barrington, while attending an outdoor meetings during the election in Mugsborough. During the campaign, 'both sides imported gangs of hired orators who held forth every night at the corners of the principal streets, and on the open spaces from portable platforms, and from motor cars and lorries'. One such freelance speaker, purchased for the cause of Sweater, the Liberal candidate, 'was a tall, slight man with dark hair, beard and moustache', whose appearance was spoiled by 'an ugly scar upon his forehead, which gave him a rather sinister appearance': "'I've seen him somewhere before", remarked Barrington, who was standing in the crowd with Harlow, Owen and Easton. "So have I", said Owen, with a puzzled expression. "But for the life of me, I can't remember where.'"

It was not until some days later that Barrington, having become separated from Owen in the election crowds, found himself listening to this same hired orator with the scar on his forehead. He observes how the speaker avoids all references to socialism. Then it dawns on him: this was the socialist speaker who had been attacked on the hill at Windley earlier in the summer. After the speaker descends from his platform, Barrington confronts him. He is, indeed, the orator who was nearly killed by a stone thrown at his head earlier in the year. The man personifies the bitterness of betrayal:

'When I devoted my life and what abilities I possess to the service of my fellow workmen; when I sought to teach them how to break their chains; when I tried to show them how they might save their children from poverty and shameful servitude, I did not want them to give me money. I did it for love. And they paid me with hatred and injury. But since I have been helping their masters to rob them, they have treated me with respect.'

The issue rested on the question of the capacity of the majority to respond to reason. (This is perhaps the most important political issue of 'the century of democracy'.) The hired Liberal bore the literal scar paid as a price for his faith in the reason of his fellow workers. Barrington responds in predictable socialist terms: 'Circumstances make us what we are; and anyhow, the children are worth fighting for.' This is more than feeble environmental determinism: it is a defence of mass rationality and the case for democratic communication, even though it might be directed towards the most unthinking and uncaring of auditors. What alternative is there to this stoical persistence in the face of adversity? The alternative is suggested in the estranged, embryonically fascistic language of the disfigured freelance orator:

'Look at them! The people you are trying to make idealists of! Look at them! Some of them howling and roaring like wild beasts, or laughing like idiots, others standing with dull and stupid faces devoid of any trace of intelligence or expression, listening to the speakers whose words convey no meaning to their stultified minds, and others gleaming with savage hatred of their fellow men, watching eagerly for an opportunity to provoke a quarrel that they may gratify their brutal natures by striking someone – their eyes are hungry for the sight of blood! Can't you see that these people, whom you are trying to make understand your plan for the regeneration of the world... are for the most part – intellectually – on level with Hottentots? The only thing they feel any interest in are beer, football, betting and – of course – one other subject. Their highest ambition is to be allowed to work. And they desire nothing better for their children! They have never had an independent thought in their lives. These are the people whom you hope to inspire with lofty ideals! You might just as well try to make a gold brooch out of a lump of dung! Try to reason with them, to uplift them, to teach them the way to higher things. Devote your whole life and intelligence to the work of trying to get better conditions for them, and you will find that they themselves are the enemy you will have to fight against.'

It is to Noonan's great credit that he articulates this position in his novel, even though his main purpose is to claim the wisdom of the social democratic alternative to working class conformity. By including this confrontation of outlooks, Noonan exhibits an intelligent recognition of the possible consequences of frustration in the struggle to communicate. He could, had he wished, have depicted the hireling as a hypocritical mercenary, and allowed Barrington to expose his thoughtless lack of principle. That would have been too easy, and is not what happens. Barrington is disconcerted by the encounter; it is as if the sense of betrayal and demoralisation is infectious: 'His conversation with the renegade seemed to have taken all the heart out of him... All his enthusiasm was gone. Like one awakened from a dream he saw the people who surrounded him in a different light.' This was not helped by seeing a mob attacking Owen, who had evidently decided to mount his own platform and proclaim the cause of socialism. Neither Barrington nor Owen are permanently disheartened by these experiences, but it is clear that Noonan himself was not prepared to dismiss on a point of faith the Le Bonist thesis (with which he almost certainly had no direct familiarity), and construct an image of public discussion which denied reality.[10]

Hamer Shawcross, the protagonist in Howard Spring's *Fame Is The Spur*, embodies other kinds of betrayal. Published in 1940, over a quarter of a century after the first, abridged publication of *The Ragged Trousered Philanthropists*, Spring's novel is still very much a product of an age when public, open-air oratory was integral to the political culture of Britain. The novel contains historical threads which connect the speaking career of Shawcross with significant moments in the history of democratic oratory. The novel begins with the burial of Shawcross' grandfather, the Old Warrior of Peterloo, who in the course of an encounter with the militia on that bloody day in 1819, acquired a sabre which became for him a symbol of the people's right to assemble and speak. That physical symbol returns repeatedly throughout the narrative: a tangible emblem of the battle for free speech which is used first as an inspiration to Hamer, then as a virtual stage prop in his display of rhetorical theatricality, and finally it is cast into the sea as a symbolic rejection of the politics of romantic gesture. That the sabre serves to connect Peterloo with the Spanish Civil War allows a sense of historical continuity to pervade the twists and turns of the complicated novel. Again, Hamer Shawcross' childhood introduction to the idea of oratory through the Methodist preaching of his father provides a sharp historical reference to the wider origins of popular ora-

10. R Tressell (Noonan), *The Ragged Trousered Philanthopists*, original 1906, republished London, 1991, pp335, 429-34, 540-7.

tory within the tradition of Wesleyan field-preaching and Sunday classes. In its treatment of the theme of free speech, *Fame Is The Spur* is pregnant with historical resonances.

Hamer Shawcross is driven to the public platform neither by lofty idealism, nor by any indolent desire to avoid conventional labour. The impetus for the young Hamer to become a preacher is a wish to be famous; seeing the effect of a Methodist parson upon his flock, the 15-year-old Hamer notes in his diary: 'I wished I was the preacher... because it must be very fine to have a great congregation in the hollow of your hand.' Long after that diary entry, when his oratory had become famous, Hamer Shawcross recalls his boyhood admiration of the preacher: 'How grand a thing this was: to be up there swaying, dominating, exhorting.' A superficial analysis of his character would conclude that, like so many other successful politicians, Shawcross simply loved the sound of his own voice. But there was more to it than that. For Hamer Shawcross the very process of communication is one of crafted manipulation. His manipulative skills are based upon the rhetorical imposition of truths upon semiconscious listeners; they are a perversion of the power to communicate openly. The story of the success of Hamer Shawcross is a record of the betrayal of democratic discourse by the power of the orator.

In contradistinction to Shawcross stand Arnold Ryerson and his blunt wife, Pen Muff. Ryerson possesses no ambition as an orator, no temperamental predisposition to sway crowds. When asked by Pen what he knows about speaking, he admits shyly that he has been taking a Sunday school class. Pen responds: "'Fat lot o' good that'll be. If you'd been in the Salvation Army, now, ranting on the street corners. That's what you want." "I'll do my best", he said stoutly.'

Arnold's best is rather pedestrian, and at his first meeting he is saved only by the presence of Pen, who can talk to the factory women in their own Yorkshire dialect. In time Ryerson 'became a familiar figure wherever trouble broke out, a steady speaker of a solid reliable sort, lacking wit, humour or any touch of brilliance, but managing nonetheless to hold most audiences by virtue of a native integrity, a sense he conveyed of utter honesty and straightness of purpose'. The novel's assumption is clear: Ryerson's integrity allows him to roam relatively inconspicuously to 'wherever he could find a platform under a roof or a street-corner for his soapbox', whereas Shawcross, a man of little or no integrity, becomes one of the most popular orators of his time. As the years pass, Ryerson, though ever loyal to his childhood friend, Hamer, cannot but see the betrayal of reason upon which the greater orator thrives. Hamer arrives in Bradford like a flash of lightning. His unique dynamism is unmistakable. What is interesting here is that the first action he proposes is to organise an open-air meeting. As late as 1940 the idea that this would be the plan of a great organiser would have made sense. His debut on the outdoor platform is a remarkable success. Before hearing him speak, Ann comments: 'It's no joke addressing an outdoor meeting. It can be horrible.' Shawcross takes speaking neither as a joke nor as a mission, but as a performance.

Like 'the renegade' in *The Ragged Trousered Philanthropists*, Shawcross is not convinced that an appeal to reason can serve to convince his listeners: 'I believe that through their hearts, not their heads, one can get their votes.' This is to be distinguished from a rhetorical appeal to both hearts and minds. Later in his career as a Labour politician, Shawcross uses this same appeal to the heart to persuade the Welsh miners to support the First World War by breaking their resolve to strike. From this we see the ambivalence of oratory as a form, dislocated from movements, interests and the content of principles. Shawcross ends up in the House of Lords as a Labour peer. Once again we are presented with the image of the working class orator as a renegade.[11]

Given the dynamic energy of open-air meetings and the variety of characters they attracted both as speakers and listeners, one might have expected more novels to feature them. By the early twentieth century street corner and park meetings were a common element of everyday social life and a main means of popular discussion. And yet their absence from most novels is conspicuous. Could it be that users of the 'higher' literary communication form were reluctant to acknowledge the unstructured discourse of a purely oral culture that was regarded as inferior to the more significant words of printed literacy? The frequent appearance of the open-air meeting in films of the first half of the century contrasts significantly with its relative invisibility in the novel. There were, however, a few exceptions. Lionel Britton's *Hunger And Love*, published in 1931, offers a rare flavour of the attraction provided by discussion grounds such as Speakers' Corner to autodidactic young workers, such as the novel's protagonist, Arthur Phelps. He begins the novel as an impoverished and humiliated wage slave in a cold and miserable greengrocer's shop, but after being sacked moves on to work as an errand boy in a bookshop, and then to other positions within the book trade. It is an un-

11. H Spring, *Fame Is The Spur*, London, 1940, pp139, 243, 254, 279, 328.

doubtedly strange novel: half Joycean stream-of-consciousness and half Dietzgenite Marxist dialectic. Much of the novel comprises deep penetration of the intricate thought process of Phelps as his mind wanders from cosmology and the atomic composition of an infinite universe to a more mundane lust for pretty women. It is this latter consideration which takes him into Hyde Park, where, as he lies on the grass, he is approached by two girls who are probably prostitutes, and is asked if he wants 'somebody to cuddle'. At this moment he is more attracted by the meetings – or, more precisely, by the spontaneous discussions stimulated by the speakers on the platforms:

'Every here and there is a platform on which a man stands up above his fellows and some score or two of men listen to him while he talks. This does not appeal to you. *Ipse dixit.* The book of words. Round the one brain is a little sea of brains... Just to be one of the crowd, and feel, without participating in it, a flow of words passing over you, is not enough. But little groups of people talk among themselves. In between the meetings. On the ground. That is more interesting. Join in if you feel inclined. Then you are part. The great human movement. Thoughts going on. You are part.'

This passage, though consistent with the eccentric composition of the 700-page novel, provides an insight into the attraction of the outdoor meeting. For the atomised and lonely urban dweller, it offered an opportunity to be a part of something. Or, alternatively, to be present, but inconspicuously non-participative. Doubting the public exhibitionism of platform combat, like many others, Phelps is attracted to the free discussion of the small gatherings which congregate around the platforms. (Such formations are regular features of the outdoor meeting tradition, and often provide the best debates in contemporary forums such as Speakers' Corner.) To the autodidact, 'craving to see some point in the process' of society, as Phelps is, this encounter with facts, figures, opinions and quotations is an introduction to a world of articulated knowledge.

Encountering a socialist, Phelps is intrigued, but discomforted:

'Disquieting blighters, these socialists. They go about trying to convert people. Every socialist I have ever met has gone about trying to convert people. And everything would be so comfortable and peaceful otherwise...

'You would have thought that Arthur needed little encouragement to rebellion. Every circumstance in one's daily life fosters it. But he did not take at all kindly to socialism...

'Socialism doesn't have to be right or wrong – what does that matter? It is the thinking that matters. They question the root of things. Two thousand million people questioning that might find out some day.'

Returning to Hyde Park, Phelps is overwhelmed by the variety of themes upon which his mind can be fed:

'Chance and necessity, determinism foreknowledge and freewill, slums and the love of God and the benefits of capitalism, existence and whether it does exist, the origin of consciousness and life, evolution and design, atheism agnosticism and belief, socialism anarchism syndicalism collectivism Marxism and the SPGB, protection and free trade, the unvarying character of human nature, the eternal necessity of poverty, wouldn't you do the same if you had the chance, you must have heads, and the flat-earth theory. Gassing. Little knots of men, sometimes a woman – very seldom; here, look at this group, yelling like hell; draw up to the outside of it, go on! edge your way in, have a go at this chap!'

He 'has a go', but is defeated by the greater knowledge and sharper wit of the other fellow. At first this dispirits Phelps, but later he arrives at the view that to have entered debate and been made to look a fool was no bad thing:

'If you hadn't made a fool of yourself you would still be just as big a fool. Only without knowing it. You make up your mind you'll have another go. What's the good of keeping your folly inside? Better have it out! Every time you make a fool of yourself – it's unpleasant at the moment, but you feel better afterwards. It does you good.

'Speaking maketh ready man, writing exact man, reading full man. As a matter of fact, this Hyde Park-Agora-Forum stunt is really very useful. One man's own mind – what we all want is the combined effect of a great number of minds.'

In this way the outdoor meetings served to provide Phelps with a gratuitous liberal education.

Britton, who was an SDF member, clearly knew Hyde Park. We know from Bonar Thompson's autobiography that he attended his meetings and donated money when *The Black Hat* was to be published (see Chapter Five). More than any other novelist (nearly all of whom have ignored Speakers' Corner), Britton captured the assertive polemicism of the place; the following passage illustrates this:

'Then here you are another day, violently and aggressively asserting that all knowledge is relative. This loud-voiced objectionable chap in front of you attacks everything you say. "Relative to what?" – Blimey, you don't know! What is it relative to? Got you beat, he says; crowing over you; you're beat! What's he mean – beat? This isn't a battle; you're trying to get ideas. He isn't trying to get ideas. He sheers off in case you recover and try to snatch victory from him.'

It is perhaps fitting that an obscure and idiosyncratic novel of the 1930s, now long out of print, contained what was in many ways the most impressive depiction of authentic open-air discussion in an age when this was a prevalent cultural form. Its finest quality as a novel is its development of the curiosity of the socially deprived and intellectually disenfranchised thinkers for whom open-air discussion was a truly liberating cultural outlet. In the midst of a chapter of rambling diversions, Britton places into Phelps' mind a thought of much significance, which it would be negligent to omit from a work on our present theme:

'An enormous and laborious process of propaganda throughout all the ages of history has made it almost impossible for anybody to discover just how he does think, what he is thinking, or to tell anyone else about it. Certainly the first step towards finding all this out and acquiring this power is through style, the way we express our thoughts: our own thoughts. It is this fact which constitutes the value – and the danger – of the common-speech theory.'[12]

A much slighter novel about open-air speaking is Reginald Moore's *The Listening World*, published in 1946. Its main relevance is its depiction of the central character, Jamie MacIntyre (known as Mac), a freelance speaker in Hyde Park, possibly based loosely upon Bonar Thompson or Angus Ogilvy. The intellectual point of the novel is rather clouded in mist, although there seem to be allusions to spiritualism as well as what is called 'Practical Christianity'. Mac seems to enjoy dominating discussion, a skill which he had once used at Speakers' Corner to compete with an older, anarchist speaker called Griddle. If the novel has any merit it is in trying to express the internal conflict within the public orator between the need to entertain and the wish to be profound:

'Wishing he could be serious, wishing that he could tell all of them that

12. L Britton, *Hunger and Love*, London, 1931, pp54, 112-3, 147, 282-3, 287.

their search for understanding, for truth, for the solace that only a belief surpassing the power of death could bestow, he began to entertain his crowd once more. He spoke quietly, caustically, calling the Houses of Parliament into the meeting with a flick of his hand, setting the government beside him as row upon row of privileged pifflers, his lips sometimes closing over his almost toothless gums in a grin of sheer devilry. His words shook the people like slight but repeated slaps.'

This tale of the inner conflicts of a speaker dependent upon collections from the crowds and his relationships with a crowd of essentially uninspiring followers says little about the power of oratory, especially because the author's attempts to give Mac profound and crucial words to utter in private result in largely inane verbiage from which a Hyde Park crowd would be fortunate to be spared.[13]

Of much more interest in relation to the atmosphere of open-air free speech is Doreen Wallace's *The Noble Savage*, published in 1945, but set in Norfolk in 1930-31. Unlike other novels referring to outdoor meetings (with the exception of Alexander Cordell's Welsh-set *Rape of the Fair Country*), this novel deals with a non-urban outdoor meeting. By the second quarter of the twentieth century the outdoor platform would have been more commonly associated with city street corners and public parks rather than village squares or open fields, but there was still undoubtedly a good deal of open-air speaking in the countryside, not least amongst agricultural labourers. Paul Howard, a local union organiser for the farm workers, appeals to the vicar of Wingrave for permission to use the Village Hall which is controlled by the church. When informed that the hall has been requested for the purpose of recruiting members of the Agricultural Workers' Union, permission is refused, despite the fact that the local Conservative Association is free to use it. 'Reckon we'll hatta meet out in the open, bein' as you don't fare to understand democracy', is Howard's response to the vicar's refusal. This is an important point: neither in this case, nor in any of the others where outdoor meetings are depicted in novels, would they be held in the open if a proper sheltered meeting place could be secured. Although open-air speaking has its advantages in terms of drawing to the platform a passing audience which had not set out to listen to a speaker's message, few speakers would by choice arrange meetings in this way.

The meeting is described by Doreen Wallace with a degree of accuracy

13. R Moore, *The Listening World*, London, 1946, p8.

which suggests that she (a farmer's wife) had direct familiarity with such events. In particular, her awareness of the speaker's concern with the weather (a perennial problem in events of this kind) and the suitability of the terrain for meeting purposes conveys a vivid accuracy. Paul Howard 'went and stood on the hump of green to see if he fancied it as a platform. "Here, do you think?", he said, "or over by the gateposts? Better the gate, perhaps, then all the people will be in front instead of round about."' The speaker's position in relation to the audience is a matter more crucial in open-air than indoor meetings, for the potentiality for a crowd to surround and take over the meeting is much greater. The account given of the meeting, including the attendance of 'the village idiot', who 'came very close and stood stock still within a yard of Paul's group, his little eyes fixed on the third button of Paul's waistcoat, his heavy face thrust forward and his mouth open', is one of the best written in an English literary tradition which provides it with little competition.[14]

Perhaps the most powerful invocation of the imagery of unregulated open-air discussion appears in the most dismal of the dystopian literary visions of the century of Nazism and Stalinism: George Orwell's *Nineteen Eighty-Four*. Wandering through the proles' reservation within totalitarian London, situated in the vicinity of St Pancras, Winston Smith, the novel's protagonist, encounters an octogenerian prole, one of 'the last links that now existed with the vanished world of capitalism'. Seeking knowledge of life before the Revolution, Winston interrogates the old prole. For the Revolution had destroyed not only freedom, but the historical memory of freedom: the sense of the ordinariness of liberty and autonomous custom. Orwell places particular emphasis upon the atrophy of idiomatic speech and folk songs, these being the symbols of an uncontained cultural sphere. Given these indicators of freedom, it is hardly surprising that the old man's memory drifts to pre-revolutionary visits to Speakers' Corner. Reminded of it by Winston's reference to the pre-revolutionary capitalists and their lackeys, the old man is spurred to remembrance:

'Now there's a word I ain't 'eard since ever so long. Lackeys! That reg'lar takes me back, that does. I recollect – oh, donkey's years ago – I used to sometimes go to 'Yde Park of a Sunday afternoon to 'ear the blokes making speeches. Salvation Army, Roman Catholics, Jews, Indians – all sorts there was. And there was one bloke – well, I couldn't give you 'is name, but a real powerful speaker 'e was. 'E didn't 'alf give it 'em.

14. D Wallace, *The Noble Savage*, London, 1945, pp8, 21-30.

"Lackeys!", 'e says, "Lackeys of the bourgeoisie! Flunkies of the ruling class!" Parasites — that was another of them. And 'yenas — 'e definitely called 'em 'yenas. Of course 'e was referring to the Labour Party, you understand.'[15]

The tragedy of the tale was not merely the destruction of the free speech remembered, but the incapacity of the teller to discuss anything at all. Asked by Winston whether he was freer in the old times than now, after the Revolution, the old man can only babble inconsequentially, as if unconnected intellectually to the kind of beings for whom words had once been weapons of rhetoric. The image of discussion rendered obsolete (so much more convincingly portrayed by Aldous Huxley in his quite different dystopian novel, *Brave New World*) is a compelling nightmare scenario. It would be the final victory of an authoritarian culture over its willing subjects. From the Victorian literary fear of open discussion emerged a modern celebration of the autodidactic will to learn through participative debate. With Orwell a new fear is raised: what if the will to seek reason through public deliberation is denied, even as a memory? It is a question which is far from fading in significance for our own times.

15. G Orwell, *Nineteen Eighty-Four*, originally published 1949, republished Harmondsworth, 1982, p76.

The Pre-Electronic Orators

WHO were these people that stood on platforms and talked to crowds? Why did they do it? What influence did their efforts have on anyone or anything? Were these merely actors without theatres, professors whom no university would invite into a lecture hall, gurus without cults — or perhaps lunatics without asylums? There have existed no training schools for open-air speakers, no fixed-term apprenticeships or diplomas in oratory. Those who mounted the platforms were appointed by themselves.

Many — perhaps most — of the open-air speakers passed into obscurity almost as soon as their feet touched the ground beneath their platforms. The liberty of unappointed and unaccountable public verbosity attracted some who were incorrigible bores, unappealing fanatics, and eccentrics whose peculiarities bordered (sometimes on the wrong side) upon irrational lunacy. That such speakers have been drawn to the outdoor platform is not a matter for historical dispute; but it does not excuse the condescending distortion by which it has sometimes been claimed that such characteristics define anyone who might feel driven or inclined to stand upon a platform in a street or a park and orate. If some open-air speakers were instantly forgettable, and many more of mediocre quality (though rarely mundane), a few of these men and women stand out as exponents of one of the great communication traditions in our social history. There are no generalisations which can usefully be made about the most able and influential outdoor orators: they ranged from proletarian autodidacts, such as Ben Tillett, who was illiterate when he commenced his platform career, to Donald Soper, who began outdoor speaking after graduating from the University of Cambridge; there were young speakers, such as Bonar Thompson, who became known as 'The Boy Orator' in his late teens, and there was Bertrand Russell, whose orations against nuclear weapons at Speakers' Corner only began when his hair was grey. Most speakers were men, but the outdoor platform was by no means a male domain, and speakers such as Marie-Louise Berneri on the anarchist platform, and Joyce Millen, Lisa Bryan and Joan Lestor on the platform of the SPGB, were in no sense excluded because of their gender. Even superficially obvious generalisations prove to be worthless. It might seem to be self-evident that speakers have been united by an exhibitionist, or at least extrovert, trait; but this is not so, for several of the finest open-air orators of this century have been essentially shy personalities whose non-platform presences have failed to conform to their larger-than-life platform *alter egos*. Equally spurious is the converse generalisation that outdoor speakers are essentially introverted characters whose burning desire to be noticed can only find an outlet upon a public platform; the speaking career of Tony Turner, whose desire to be noticed and applauded was met in other spheres than oratory, disproves facile theories of the platform as a device for assertiveness training.

The two speakers whose pre-electronic oratory will be examined in this chapter made their marks as great orators in the 1930s, although both of them began speaking before then. It was in that decade that both speakers could be found in the same place (Speakers' Corner) attracting crowds of many hundreds, many of whom were in attendance precisely because they knew that these speakers were there. In short, they had created reputations as open-air orators. The 1930s were a period for carving stellar reputations: it was the age of the first film stars, of music hall and radio personalities, of political demagogues and individuals who seemed to personify in themselves either the safety of the last century or the excitement of the new one. The 1930s were, in one sense, a golden age of the outdoor platform. By then urban life was the norm, and the open-air meeting is largely an urban phenomenon. It was in the 1930s that political debate reached a level of mass popularity. Radio as a technology of mass discussion was still in its infancy, but most people still found the park and street corner meeting a more accessible forum for live debate than pre-scripted radio discussions involving rather stuffy and remote intellectuals whose pontifications brooked no interruptions. Most importantly, the 1930s were a period of profound ideological uncertainty: it was the age of popular enchantment with some ideas and disenchantment with others, and a sense of newly-educated excitement on the part of large numbers of literate workers as to their part in determining the course of history. If in the 1830s the mass of the people fought for the right to speak so that a minority could have the vote, by the 1930s the majority not only possessed the vote and the freedom to speak, but believed that through speaking and then voting (as well as more militant political actions) the future could be moulded to their requirements. It is for this reason that the 1930s can be regarded as the coming of age of the outdoor platform, and that the speakers considered here are both, though products of much else as well, outcomes of the cultural production of that most dramatic of decades.

☆ ☆ ☆

Bonar Thompson, arguably the most impressive of all the Hyde Park orators, belonged to a sub-culture within the cultural sphere of the open-air medium in that he was a freelance orator, a person who spoke not for principles, but for payment by the crowd. As he put it in his autobiography, *Hyde Park Orator*, published in 1934:

'By 1930 I was established in Hyde Park as the leading freelance speaker. I had gathered round me an audience which knew me and understood something of my attitude. These choice and master spirits would tolerate no interference of any kind with their right to listen to their favourite speaker. It was generally understood that I could do no wrong. Everyone had to accept me as an orator unique among public speakers. I had no policy, no programme and no plan, no wish to uplift anybody, no concern for any social or political problem, and no message for humanity. I spoke on any subject, or no subject. Sometimes I put forward two mutually exclusive points of view in the same speech, and won general approval.'[1]

The function of these performances of public eloquence were not dissimilar to those of the medieval *vagi scolares*, and, like them, Bonar Thompson attempted no disguise as to the purpose of his speaking:

'It must not be imagined that I thank those who cheer or contribute to the collection. They are paying for services rendered — that is all. I am entitled to whatever they give, and much more than I imagine any of them have ever thought of giving. I owe them nothing. The boot is on the other foot.'[2]

As a freelance speaker, accountable only to the harshest of free market forces, performing a kind of oratorical prostitution, Bonar Thompson recognised that, whilst being much admired, he was in an ultimately undignified position, dependent upon the voluntary payments of the crowd, and regarded with contempt within the ranks of the outdoor orators:

1.   B Thompson, *Hyde Park Orator*, London, 1934, p94.
2.   Ibid.

'The fate of the freelance speaker is in the hands of the capricious multitudes, fickle and feather-brained, who will lap up his eloquence like dogs and leave him to starve in the end. He has to compete with the half-witted and lunatic speakers who... naturally draw the largest crowds. To a shallow public, who try to look intelligent, and fail, he pours out the treasures of his mind. He has no status. He receives no tangible recognition for his services. He bears the stigma of the Hyde Park tub-thumper, even though he has never thumped a tub in his life. He is the outcast of the oratorical world, the Ishmael of politics and the prey of time. The profession of a speaker who cuts himself adrift from the herd, who cannot submit his intelligence to the rule of a party, is a blind alley. He must die worn out and unwept, soon forgotten.'[3]

The fact is that Bonar Thompson could not make up his mind about himself. He knew that he was one of the most successful open-air orators of his age, admired and supported by many thousands, but his egotistical self-regard was always fragile; he could not decide whether the ability to speak for money mattered very much, or whether those by whom his ego was supported were worthy judges of talent. He felt that his career was possibly pointless, but conceivably a form of durable artistic talent, and his insecurity gave rise to a form of cynicism by which he affected amoral indifference to his listeners and his own performance. This affectation bordered upon the fascistic, with Bonar Thompson expressing extreme disdain towards the crowds who followed him and the class from which they came.

He came from County Antrim in Ulster, where he was born in Carnearney, near to Ballymena, in 1888. An illegitimate child, he was brought up by a strictly puritanical aunt from whom he learnt of the dangers posed by frivolous amusements, which included all music other than hymns, and book reading. As a child, Bonar Thompson, known then as Johnny, dreamed of becoming a great preacher. The greatest influence on him then was his uncle Bonar, known locally as something of an oracle and story-teller. 'He was feared for his erudition and his sharp tongue', according to his nephew's memoirs. Another influence upon him was his friend, Billy O'Neil, a fiddle player of some repute. Young Bonar Thompson's earliest encounter with an orator of any sort was Samuel Owens, a local octogenarian poet who composed political odes which outraged his loyalist Ulster audiences; in the year of Victoria's Jubi-

3. Ibid, p247.

lee Bonar Thompson recalls Owens 'standing upon a stone at the foot of Carnearney mountain... chanting an ode specially written by him for the occasion, while the village youths pelted him with manure, clods of earth, pieces of turf and other missiles'. Walking eight miles to the town of Antrim, young Bonar Thompson heard Owens disrupt a church service by reciting a politically contentious poem as a vote of thanks to the preacher. It was in Antrim that he first saw the street performers whose command of the crowd amazed the onlooking country boy.

At the age of nearly 14, Bonar Thompson went to live with his mother and her new husband in Oliver Street, Manchester. He commenced employment for the Great Central Railway as an oiler and greaser in the carriage and wagon department. These four years of conventional employment were to be the longest period in which Bonar Thompson worked for an employer. For it was in Manchester that he discovered a new means of living: the open-air platform and collections taken from audiences. At the age of 17, he first discovered Stevenson Square where, on Sundays, outdoor meetings had become a well-established tradition. Bonar Thompson was enthralled:

'I had never seen anything of the kind before, and was immensely interested by the speakers. It seemed a wonderful thing to me that these men should be able to hold the attention of the crowds in the way they were doing. Practically all the arguments that were being used were beyond my comprehension, but I felt that great affairs were under way... I resolved to attend the Square every Sunday until I had plucked out the heart of the mystery that lay behind the high-sounding phraseology of the orators.'[4]

In this response, Bonar Thompson was typical. For many thousands of uneducated and semi-educated workers, the stimulus to autodidactic self-improvement was first engendered by an encounter with the platform. The orators were workers whose very words and diction seemed to raise them above their peers; many would quote books, stanzas of verse and scholarly aphorisms. The desire of listeners to become part of this higher learning, all the more attractive because it was neither imposed nor controlled, was enormous. The function of the outdoor platform in the generations immediately following the first Education Acts as literal open universities and colleges of shared experience has been too frequently neglected. Sometimes there were elements of pomposity in the public ver-

4.   Ibid, pp72-3.

bosity of these worker-intellectuals, and, as Bonar Thompson suggests, somewhat bitterly, the presence of a certain amount of cant and theatricality was often discernible from the platforms, but this does not diminish the effect that such speech-making had in giving confidence to listeners who would never otherwise have believed that wisdom could come from the mouths of people like themselves. Bonar Thompson's response to what he heard was to read whatever he could. He preferred William Morris, Daniel De Leon and Jack London to Marx, whom he regarded as a 'giant bore'. Perhaps the attraction of these writers was that they were all open-air speakers, and in the first two cases their writings were virtual transcripts of their speeches. It was not long before Bonar Thompson made what was to be the most important decision in his life: 'I resolved to become a speaker. To sway masses, to dominate crowds, to hear the applause — here was an easy road to fame. More than that, it was a chance to escape from poverty and hard, irksome, badly paid labour.'[5]

In reality what he did was to swap a life of wage slavery for one of impoverished dependence upon coins solicited from crowds. It is dubious whether Bonar Thompson's claimed reason for becoming a speaker, written in a mood of some bitterness, and with a style of unbecoming affectation of amorality, can be entirely trusted. Another reason given by him for becoming a speaker is perhaps rather more plausible:

'At work and at my lodgings I was a nobody. I could not assert or express myself. I had no proper education, no social gifts, no powers of speech. I was a dumbbell. So that in choosing to become a speaker I was seeking both to escape from hard work and to find a means of exploiting my inborn histrionic talents.'[6]

His first speech in Stevenson Square, largely concocted from phrases found in socialist pamphlets, lasted for half an hour and met with great applause. Before long Bonar Thompson became known as 'The Boy Orator'. He spoke each Sunday, and attended meetings at the County Forum (see Chapter Three), where he encountered some of the great speakers of the day, the finest of whom, in his opinion, was the syndicalist, Tom Mann. Before leaving Manchester, Bonar Thompson served a year in Strangeways prison for his part in an act of conspiracy (a shop window was smashed to draw attention to the plight of the unemployed) which he later claimed was merely a stunt to make himself a martyr so that more

5.   Ibid, p78.
6.   Ibid.

people would respect him as a radical speaker and give him money. In 1909, at the age of 22, Bonar Thompson walked from Manchester to London. His destination was Hyde Park and he addressed his first meeting there on the day of his arrival. From then until the outbreak of war in 1914 he held three meetings every Sunday, and at least one on most other days. On the average Sunday he would receive collections of 10 shillings. As well as in Hyde Park he spoke at all the major prewar speaking stations: Highbury Corner; Finsbury Park; Brockwell Park; Victoria Park; Peckham Rye; Clapham Common; Parliament Hill Fields; Jack Straw's Castle, Hampstead; The World's End, Chelsea; Jolly Butcher's Hill, Wood Green; Beresford Square, Woolwich; Golden Square, Soho; Catherine Street, Croydon; and Howland Street, off Tottenham Court Road.

Speaking first as an anarchist and then, for one year, as a member of the British section of the Industrial Workers of the World, and then after the war for two years on the 'open socialist' platform, Bonar Thompson decided in the mid-1920s to establish his own platform. Describing himself as 'an unattached speaker, a freelance, reserving the right to support or oppose any party or no party', his reputation as an orator came increasingly to depend upon an Oscar Wilde-like ability to utter witty aphorisms and cast sardonic reflections upon the misplaced piety of idealists and the crass hypocrisy of the governing elite. Michael Foot recalls that he 'quickly became an addict' of Bonar Thompson's oratory. In the midst of the strident ideological confusions which abounded in the 1930s, 'Bonar Thompson's scepticism was, I suppose, the sanest thing in the land', wrote Foot: 'Certainly he was the most innocent citizen of the whole metropolis; he never did anybody any harm and did nameless, countless multitudes plenty of good.'[7] Bonar Thompson would amuse his listeners with witty observations, such as: 'Half the misery in the world is caused by ignorance. The other half is caused by knowledge.' Of militarism he said: 'When a monarch, a president, a premier or other national leader announces that he will fight to the death, he is generally in dead earnest. He is referring, of course, not to his own death – but yours.' Such comments were produced in a self-produced magazine called *The Black Hat*, which had a brief and eccentric existence thanks to financial support from some of Bonar Thompson's greatest admirers, including Sean O'Casey and John Galsworthy. As well as speaking in Hyde Park and the numerous metropolitan outdoor speaking locations, Bonar Thompson travelled to Glasgow, where he spoke on the Green, and Newcastle, where he set up

7. M Foot, *Debts of Honour*, London, 1980, pp109-15.

his platform in the Bigg Market. On his travels he attempted to utilise his speaking talents as a market salesman, selling books about contraception – even though he had a moral objection to birth control.

Bonar Thompson had an exceptional ego. He proclaimed frequently from his platform that most of what he knew he learned from listening to himself speak on the outdoor platform. 'Speakers ape and copy each other continually', he wrote, 'but no one has ever been able to imitate me, either as speaker or entertainer.' Comparing himself to Shakespeare (although conceding that the latter's name would endure beyond his), he claimed to have 'raised the intellectual and artistic standard of public speaking and taught the frequenters of Hyde Park that a man can work in a low, disreputable and despised medium and still create something from it that has an element of worth'. In fact, Bonar Thompson wanted more than that: he sought fame and money, but became, at best, a well-known practitioner of an undignified communication form, and he certainly never obtained more money than he needed to live a meagre existence. He was invited to broadcast on BBC radio (a medium that was to play its part in the demise of the open-air meeting), but, with the exception of a few invitations to universities and exclusive debating clubs, Bonar Thompson's recognition was confined to the parks and streets.

Oddly enough, for a man so dependent financially and, it would seem, psychologically, upon his audiences, Bonar Thompson had a bitter disdain for the crowds who surrounded him. Perhaps this was a compensatory claim for his knowledge that he was at their mercy. Members of the crowd who asked him questions particularly annoyed him: 'Questions break the spell of a meeting and do the speaker no good at collection-time. The crowd becomes so interested in the stupid questions – all questioners are stupid – they would not be questioners if they were not – that they forget all about the speaker's need to live.'[8]

Worse than questioners were 'bores': those members of the crowd who wanted to talk to the speaker after the meeting was over. He wrote: 'The trite remarks, commonplace observations, and the banal and stupid chatter of the thousands of people who have insisted on conversing with me outside the gates of Hyde Park have contributed substantially towards the ruin of my nervous system.'[9] Was this contempt mere arrogance? Or might it have been the insecurity of a merchant of oratory who, like the street prostitute who maintains as untouchable one part of her anatomy,

8. Thompson, op cit, p116.
9. Ibid, p116, see also p160.

had to maintain some distance from those who paid for his greatness; had they been allowed too close, perhaps the greatness would have emerged as a verbal illusion. There is something more than a little odd about Bonar Thompson's professed detestation of 'the great big blubbering, bullying, chuckle-headed mob' who provided him with his living. There is more than a touch of Le Bon in his comment: 'My experience of crowds has taught me to despise them, and a few years in London... destroyed my faith in the masses and almost convinced me of the probable ultimate collapse of the human mind.'[10]

The contrast between the two Hyde Park speakers, Bonar Thompson and Donald Soper, appears to be almost complete. The former a virtual vagrant dependent upon coins from collections, the latter a highly-esteemed Methodist Minister, one-time President of the Methodist Conference and member of the House of Lords; the former a relentless sceptic, acerbically defiant of even the secular certainties of atheist dogma, the latter a highly committed Christian for whom the practical establishment of the Kingdom of God has guided his mission as an orator; the former a man of no professed principles and a detestation of those who did profess them, the latter a man whose speaking has been inseparable from declarations of principled commitments to not only religion, but also socialist and pacifist ideals; the former a speaker for whom the listening crowd was at best a tediously ever-present paymaster, the latter a preacher dedicated to the salvation of his crowd whom he has regarded less as spectators than witnesses of a transformative Word. While Soper and Bonar Thompson could and often did draw the same people to their audiences, the experience of hearing their oratory would be dramatically different in each case; it is important to recognise that within the communication tradition of the open-air platform one need only walk a matter of yards from one platform to another to encounter a totally different purpose for the practice of discourse.

Donald Soper has been a notably dignified outdoor orator. This dignity does not emanate from obvious sources: his title of honour, his dog collar or the refinement of his accent; these in themselves count for little. Soper has brought dignity to the open-air platform, in marked contradistinction to the mercenary character of the freelance speakers such as Bonar Thompson, because he has utilised a remarkable vocabulary, ele-

10. Ibid, p198.

gance of expression and profound wit in the service of a burning desire to win listeners to beliefs which otherwise, stated in the same forum in the absence of such qualities, could well have been dismissed as the rantings of a crank. Soper has dignified radical eccentricity, and in so doing has made it more difficult for the opponents of open discussion to deride it as an undignified medium.

The totality of the contrast between Soper and Bonar Thompson only appears to be the case. In fact, both men had a strictly puritanical up- bringing which did much to influence their lives as speakers. The demo- cratic tendencies implicit within the austere puritan tradition have played a major role, not just in the twentieth century, in nurturing a participa- tive and critical approach to communication. (This can be particularly observed in America where the relationship between the Protestant free- preaching of the founding fathers and the huge cultural spread of the Lyceums, lecture halls and stump orators in the nineteenth and early twentieth centuries was intimate.) Just as Bonar Thompson's harsh in- fancy in Protestant rural Ulster did still allow him to be exposed to heck- ling in the church at Antrim, so Donald Soper was born into a family of seemingly stifling puritanical emotional austerity, but one nonetheless in which the nonconformist principles of reading, moral discussion and re- spect for the meaning of words were actively encouraged.

Born in 1903 to middle class parents in Knoll Road, Wandsworth, in London, Donald Soper was the son of a City of London average adjuster who was also a Methodist lay preacher, and a mother who was a teacher. He was exposed to little beyond the narrowness of a catechismic culture of Methodism. Whilst still a schoolboy, at Aske's in Hatcham, he agreed to his father's wish that he should become a Minister. In September 1926 he became one, but not without a period of extreme introspective doubt dur- ing his period as an Exhibitioner at St Catherine's College, Cambridge, where, in the course of his first-year studies, he read Lecky's *History of Rationalism*, and became for a brief time a committed atheist. Despite being a confident student – sometimes to the point of arrogance – and an outstanding scholar, Soper suffered from depression, in part the result of bad health, but also a consequence of two tragedies which he had endured: the death of his brother, and a sporting accident at school in which he had fast- bowled a cricket ball to another boy and fatally injured him.

Donald Soper began his period as a probationer Minister at the South London Methodist Mission in the Old Kent Road, where his encounter with the poverty of working class life shocked him and served as an early revelation, giving rise to his commitment to the ideal of socialism. It was during a missionary visit to a railway works in Derby at this time that he resolved, in a moment of apparent revelation, to become a professed socialist. He has stated: 'You cannot... follow Jesus Christ unless you accept his teaching, as well as seek to be inspired by his spirit. And the teaching of Jesus Christ seems to me to be inevitably linked with socialism.' In a BBC broadcast in 1965, he explained: 'The foundation of my socialist belief is that I regard socialism as the economic and political expression, in time, of what I believe to be the Kingdom of God.' Guided by this belief, he speaks not only as a Methodist but as a member of the Labour Party; the latter he regards as being less than socialist in its policies, and the former he regards as being the higher motive for addressing the multitude: 'There is much more in Christianity than in socialism.'

He began to speak on the outdoor platform in 1926, while still a probationer at the South London Mission:

'One day a young fellow of my congregation, who worked in the City, came to me much exercised in his mind. He went each dinner time to Tower Hill, and among the various speakers to whom he listened he was as impressed by the incisive and the measured arguments of the Catholic Evidence Guild as he was dissatisfied with the fatuous and petulant explosions of the many so-called Protestant advocates. Was there not an intellectual case for the faith which he heard from the Methodist pulpit Sunday by Sunday? Could not we defend the things dear to us reasonably and persuasively? He was sure that he spoke for many others who felt that much religious propaganda on the Hill was a waste of time and most ineffectively done... Would I have a go at it? I readily agreed. We promised to meet on the next Tuesday. Had I known as much of the Hill as I do now I should probably not have agreed so glibly to put matters right.'[11]

He arrived at Tower Hill, as promised, but had no idea how to start a meeting. He was advised to climb on to the wall which surrounds the speaking area. He did so, but no audience was drawn. He was then advised to clap his hands, after doing which a crowd began to assemble. When he commenced by declaring the religious intention of the meeting the crowd dispersed, and the occasion was only saved by the arrival of a Marxist critic, whose objection to Soper's 'opium of the people' enabled the speaker to pursue a course of oratory which was never to cease for the

11. Interview with the author, October 1993.

remainder of his life. By the beginning of the 1930s Soper was running regular meetings at Tower Hill, Highbury Corner (then a very popular speaking station in Islington) and Speakers' Corner, where his Sunday meetings beneath Reformer's Tree became established as a form of open-air evangelism unique in its successful attempt to make religious thought accessible to a secular audience.

Still speaking regularly at both Speakers' Corner and Tower Hill at the time of writing, Soper, at the age of 94, has been able to offer some enlightening thoughts about the function of open-air meetings and his motives for becoming a speaker in such an environment. 'I very soon discovered', he explained, 'that the Church is too busy answering the questions it thinks people ought to be asking, but rather it's much more important to start where they are, with questions people ask.'[12] It is this agenda-setting role of the crowd and the interactive nature of the communication involved which makes the outdoor platform a far more communicative medium for Soper than are newspapers or television:

'The casual use of the newspaper means that you touch on a number of subjects, but unless you're diligent you're not inclined to dwell on any of them; whereas if you're persistently asked a question in the open air, then you can have some kind of fellowship of controversy in an area of mutual concern. That is the quality... that really makes up a worthwhile meeting: that you contradict one another or comment on one another, and there's no difficulty about questioning. Television can't compete with Speakers' Corner in a fellowship of controversy. It can only make a proclamation or give an edited occasion which is never... spontaneous and hasn't got the sparkle, the reality. The problem today is making sense of such a proliferation of ideas and statements and trying to get to the core of matters which is only possible... when you have a protracted opportunity of discussion.'[13]

Soper does not regard himself as an innovator: 'The Methodist tradition is open-air speaking.' In defending it he explains: 'It's the one kind of expression of the Christian faith which enables the statements that are made to be immediately under correction or explication. There's an immediacy about the open-air.' Indeed, he compares this immediacy of debate to the verbal discussions between Jesus and those whom he encountered, as described in the New Testament. The sanctity of this tradition

12. Ibid.
13. Ibid.

does not prevent Soper from recognising the tendency towards a degree of showmanship by orators such as himself: 'I can remember one of the earliest questions I was asked was, "What's the shape of your soul when you're dead?", and I told him "oblong" and it seemed to satisfy him.' This uneasy balance between a sacred mission and a public performance is the price to be paid for reaching and holding a crowd. It is a task in which Soper has persisted even during the most precarious days, such as the war years when, as a pacifist, he continued speaking throughout the blitz, vulnerable to the attacks of servicemen who objected to his moral stance, and the blasts of German bombs. (One blew a book from his hand as he was speaking on the platform in the early 1940s.)

Whilst asserting that the inherent root of human violence emanates from what he believes to be the original sin of Man, Soper is no less vociferous in his rejection of the Bible as a totalitarian intellectual cudgel. Preceding more recent trends in liberal theology by decades, as early as the 1930s Soper was denying in public the literal fundamentalism of his more dogmatic co-religionists and building his reputation as a communicator upon a capacity for self-expression, without resort to the simplistic sloganeering of the more self-parodying saviours of souls. It was through this quality, and his expression of radical beliefs which appeased the reason of his secularist listeners, that Soper became one of the most popular and respected of the pre-electronic orators.

☆   ☆   ☆

The impressions made by these speakers upon the many thousands who listened to them, and the effects achieved by their oratory, are difficult to identify simply. To many they will have provided little more than free entertainment (only optionally free in the case of Bonar Thompson and his fellow freelance orators). The significant role of the open-air meeting in the history of popular leisure in the days before the rise of broadcasting has yet to be adequately recorded. FW Batchelor observed:

'... the nearest approach to the Old Time Variety Show at the present time can be seen and heard at Marble Arch's "Orator's Corner" any Sunday – what a program! Serious artists, Comedy, Free Lance Speakers... and it starts at 11am or before, and is non-stop till 11pm. Nothing to pay, fresh air, refreshments just across the road, and if you go often enough you will get to know all the artists and where your favourites will appear and at what time.'

Then there is the educative function provided, particularly valuable in a period when most adults left school in their mid-teens, and opportunities for serious discussion and debate for the formally uneducated were few. This was also noted by Batchelor:

'I venture to say that more knowledge can be gleaned on international and political affairs in one hour on any Sunday, than can be obtained from reading newspapers all the week. These speakers know their subjects; are well read and keep themselves up to date on the latest vital European situations as they arise (which unfortunately they do from day to day). Listening to them are hundreds of people, intellectual and well dressed, or otherwise.'[14]

The speakers' ability to 'know their subjects' comprised more than a *claim* to expertise, rather like the TV captions which label 20-second speakers as 'Expert on the Middle East' or 'Market Specialist'. It was an ability which had to be manifested over long hours and tested by interrogations characterised often by knowledge and wit, as well as a good deal of frivolity and superficiality. The speaker who could not sustain his or her case simply would not last in an interactive setting, and would either have to give up, or, like one speaker in the 1970s who recited the Lord's prayer every time his argument was interrupted, retreat into the communicative impotence of monologue.

It was in the course of this 'testing' of speakers, which has sometimes appeared as a relentless, sadistic determination by the crowd to puncture the insolence of anyone who claims to know anything, that the most significant role of the public meeting emerged. Here was a chance for people not merely to favour democracy, but to practise what it means to be democratic. From this experience of being democratic, some went on to join parties and movements, to become speakers themselves, or to rehearse arguments they had learned in different settings. Others could simply claim that they had witnessed what it is to hear fine speaking, to discriminate between good oratory and bad, and between sense and nonsense in debate, and to realise that deliberation on great matters was for anyone with a mind to speak. Whether listening to or arguing with a member of the House of Lords and past leader of the Methodist Church or a rhetorical performer who, had chances of birth and upbringing been different, may well have been orating in a different place, the chance afforded to speakers and listeners alike to bear democratic witness was uniquely edifying and civilising.

14. FW Batchelor, *Around The Marble Arch: Wit And Humour of the Hyde Park Orators*, London, 1939.

From Oratory to Oprah: The Twilight of Public Discussion

PARADOXICALLY, it was the aftermath of victory in the 'War To Save Democracy' which set the scene for the erosion of open-air, uncontrolled, free and public discussion in Britain. It is true that fascism was defeated, even if it was at the cost of allowing Stalin, 'our democratic ally', to confine more of Europe within dictatorial rule than had been the case in 1939. But the defeat of Hitler's anti-democratic tyranny abroad by no means guaranteed the health of a more democratic culture at home. Indeed, the centralised state powers made necessary by war, the secretive and manipulative control of information (and disinformation), the consensual force for the suppression of dissent, and a growing military technology of official communication gave many people in authority a taste for the continuation of such regulation in a period of peace. As far as democratic culture was concerned, the most important social change between 1926, when the government beat the General Strike with the aid of its own propaganda press backed up by the new medium of radio, and 1946, the first full year of peace, was that in the intervening years the state had developed an unprecedentedly potent institution for the formation of mass opinion: the BBC, officially established in 1922, but only confirmed as the Voice of the Nation during the Second World War.

The demise of public discussion did not occur immediately. In fact, it was preceded by an illusory flowering of popular debate. Although street and park discussion had been constrained during the war, with dissent always voiced in the memory of the draconian sanctions of the last world war, it *had* existed: off-duty servicemen continued to congregate at Speakers' Corner and other well-known sites to hear how it was that they were wasting their time fighting for capitalism (from Turner), or that to kill under any circumstances was sinful (from Soper). With the conclusion of the war a number of factors appeared to favour extended public discussion.

Firstly, there was the widespread experience of open debate within the armed forces, particularly in the final days of the war. As early as August

1941 WE Williams was charged with directing the newly-formed Army Bureau of Current Affairs (ABCA). This body not only provided educational bulletins for use in adult education for the servicemen, but facilitated widespread discussions within training time – discussions which increasingly took more of the form of prewar street meetings than officer-led indoctrination. Well might one distinguished Oxford academic have commented that 'there had not been an army in England which discussed like this one since that famous Puritan Army which produced the Putney Debates and laid the foundation of modern democracy'. At its peak in 1943, no less than 62 123 lectures were given to the troops by civilian speakers – and not all of these were politically innocuous. As thousands of servicemen awaited demobilisation and return to civil life at the end of the war, they found themselves beneficiaries of informed lectures and vibrant debates organised by ABCA. Despite a temptation to romanticise it, this had indeed been a 'people's war' in which for many volunteers and conscripts the fight against fascism and all it signified meant also a fight for democratic values of a nature wider than that embraced by Churchill and his class. If for many this objective had been hazy and unarticulated, ABCA provided a forum to work out what democracy might mean. This process led some to see themselves as collective parts of an essentially neutral state, whilst others drew a distinction between the passivity of parliamentary representation and the participative necessity of an active democratic culture. Ironically, although those promoting ABCA endorsed the former view, the form which this self-educational discussion frequently took pointed more towards Speakers' Corner than the bombast of the House of Commons.

Secondly, the physical effects of the war upon the urban landscape made suitable places for outdoor meetings more numerous. Bomb sites were ideal for public oratory. One, close to Manchester's Victoria Station, was so popular that when the land was finally developed for office building the new block was – and is still – called Speakers' House.

Thirdly, the general election of 1945 generated a degree of excitement and public involvement which was exceptional. It took place during a period of good weather, and was to a considerable degree fought on the hustings in the streets. Both Churchill and Bevan (the finest orators of their respective parties) spent more time on the outdoor platform than on the radio. Not only the major political parties, but smaller ones such as the Common Wealth Party (which won its first and only seat in 1945), the Communist Party (which won two seats) and the Socialist Party of

Great Britain (which contested its first general election, in Paddington North) made substantial impacts, quite disproportionate to their membership numbers, simply on the strength of persistent and persuasive oratory. No serious research has been carried out on the degree to which the Tories' relative inexperience in these rough-and-tumble circumstances contributed to their alienation from the voters, and to their massive loss of seats. The postwar years were a brief moment of untypically British celebration of the very forms of ordinary speech which had hitherto been ignored or derided: newsreel presenters imitated northern and cockney cheerful matter-of-factness; Ministry of Information films carefully excluded tones of Etonion condescension, and sought cultural salvation in diversities of speech and style; it was the voice of the music hall and not the gentlemen's club which seemed to have won the war. And with Labour's landslide election victory in July 1945 there was much to suggest that the democracy of the streets would flourish, perhaps even in a new form as a legitimised part of British political culture. After all, it was to secure the right to argue freely in public that the war had been fought — or so it was said.

The postwar revival of street and park meetings was not to last. They represented a return to a form of unofficial democratic communication which had enjoyed its peak in the last two decades of the nineteenth century and the prewar years of the twentieth. Postwar society was to be dominated by new forms of communication, and obstacles to the old ones. The obstacles were no longer legal ones; the ghosts of Peterloo and Bloody Sunday were buried, but new, less romantic barriers to uncontrolled speech emerged. Of these the most obvious and irritating to outdoor speakers was the increase of traffic. As more people took to the road, the noise of motor cars and their intrusion into previously open spaces made it increasingly less congenial for crowds to gather on street corners. Where once platform orators had to compete at worst with drunken disrupters and Salvation Army bands, the roar of passing buses, lorries and cars was now drowning out the sound of the human voice. In London, the best illustration of this effect was the cessation of the regular outdoor meetings at Whitestone Pond in Hampstead, which in the 1930s and 1940s had been vigorous and influential locally, but died out in the early 1950s due to the site being next to the convergence of three busy, noisy roads. The two most revolutionary changes in postwar communication were the spread of motorised transport and mass radio broadcasting. The former diminished people's sense of space, made it possible to travel without great preparation, and created a perception of local landmarks such as parks and street corners as parochial. Radio transformed the way that large groups of people pursued discussion. Although at first radio broadcasts were often listened to by crowds outside wireless shops or by groups who would listen and then discuss what the invisible speakers had told them, this trend was not to last beyond 1934 when the BBC's Central Council for Broadcast Adult Education (CCBAE) was finally closed down.[1] Radio introduced the one-way conversation, the listener reduced to a degree of passivity alien to the function of practical communication. Professional interlocutors, hand-picked for their inoffensive neutrality, were placed in studios and permitted on occasions to ask questions of speakers on behalf of the listening audience. Often the audience was denied even that: radio transmitted talks by selected experts whose words were offered solely for immediate consumption, but were never open to the possibility of interruption or the scrutiny of lay questioning. The voices offered were condensed in comparison to previous communication forms. Whereas open-air oratory could last for hours, and organised public meetings in halls were comprised of speeches often lasting for an hour followed by periods for questions and discussion, radio squeezed its words into relatively brief time slots so that it would be rare to hear a talk containing as many words as an average quality newspaper article. So, with the spread of radio throughout the country — a development stimulated by the war and the cheapness of the technology — which was soon followed by the even more pervasive growth of television consumption, people were hearing and seeing new and more elaborate words and images, but found themselves less actively involved in the activity of communication. They were being communicated to; discourse gave way to the spectacle. Anthony Smith, in *The Shadow In The Cave* (probably the best analysis of British radio broadcasting), states well the nature of the transformation in communication which mass broadcasting entailed:

'... if there is only one soapbox available, or one megaphone or one printing press (or at best a limited number of them), to whom should they be lent: to the man who fights to the front of the queue, or to the man who in the opinion of some independent body has the most interesting things to say? Our society inherits a belief in the benefits of free discussion on the grounds that only through it can society reach the most logically ordered, the best-argued decisions... In a society in which the

1. M Pegg, *Broadcasting and Society, 1918-39*, London, 1983, p167.

decision-takers number millions, in fact the entire adult population, it is impossible for everyone to take part as anything more than a member of an inert audience.'[2]

Of course, the problem never was that there was only one 'soapbox'. The intrinsic democracy of that form of discussion is that plurality is guaranteed; if you wish to compete with what the orator says you may question, heckle or put up your own platform a short distance away. Nobody is confined to inertia until the technology of producing one-way communication, and the airwaves through which they are transmitted, are owned and controlled by the state — or by anyone at all, for that matter.

With the rise of radio came the professionalisation of speaking. The long process of liberating the working class voice by letting it be heard and respected within its own medium was set back by the pervasive dominance of 'BBC English' against which unofficial speakers could be downgraded or dismissed. (The BBC's Advisory Committee on Spoken English, set up in 1926 under the stewardship of A Lloyd James, was at pains to ensure that the common ear was to be addressed by far from 'common' speech.) The discussion of philosophical and social topics through such BBC radio institutions as *The Brains Trust* conveyed an unmistakable message that serious discussion was the province of the great and the good. Trained minds would train the minds of the listener, fortunate indeed to be the inert recipient of such edifying one-way conversations. The professionalism of the speakers served to accentuate the feeble amateurishness of the listeners. Studio audiences were permitted to clap, and, where wit was offered in comprehensible enough forms for their consumption, to laugh with polite restraint.

With noisier postwar streets and a seductive new relationship of one-way discussion with their radio and television sets, it is little wonder that fewer people bothered to attend open-air meetings. By the 1950s most organisations and speakers dependent upon this form were complaining that audiences were dwindling. The outdoor meeting was coming to be seen as an anachronism, best confined to 'traditional' speaking areas.

One other reason for this decline is rather ironic. Fascism was associated in most people's minds with the swaying of crowds by mob orators. They did not need to see newsreel footage of the rallies at Nuremberg to perceive this, but could recall in many cases the open-air meetings of Mosley and the British Blackshirts. Mosley's fascistic Union Party con-

2. A Smith, *The Shadow in the Cave: The Broadcaster, the Audience and the State*, London, 1976, p50.

tinued to hold outdoor meetings in London and elsewhere in the postwar years. The defining characteristics of these meetings, which placed them outside of the open-air speaking tradition as it has been examined here, were the absence of interaction between speakers and audiences, and the presence of ritualistic exhibitions of sloganeering and quasi-militarism. Despite the cultural exceptionalism of this kind of outdoor meeting, the experience of fascism and the simplified Le Bonist analyses that were often used to explain its mass appeal served to some extent to tar all open-air oratory. Might not all speakers standing above a crowd on a platform be frustrated little Mussolinis or Hitlers waiting for their chance? Did not all crowds, however cerebral their interaction with a speaker, constitute potential regiments of brainwashed followers? The suggestion was never made explicit, but neither was it possible for everyone to exorcise the linking images.

Ironically, though, it was radio and cinema, the newly-embraced and respectable communication media, which had been most successfully adopted in the cause of the fascist assault upon reason. The new mass media colonised popular discussion. When once a working man or woman might have spent a few hours each week participating vocally in public debate, now it was more comfortable to listen in to somebody else's debate. But radio offered more than discussion. Indeed, as the electronic media have developed, the tendency has been less to provide an alternative form of discussion than to offer an alternative to discussion. The diversions of entertainment have come increasingly not simply to supplement rational discussion (which they always had from music halls to *ITMA*), but to replace it. There are many reasons for this, not least of which relates to a genuine consumer demand for easy amusement. Given the passionate resistance of those with power to working class self-articulation and democratic discussion, it is easy to drift towards conspiracy theories which explain the diversionary function of the tranquillising babble which comprises much of what now passes for mass entertainment. None shall be offered here. Neither Huxleyesque intentions to sedate the restless masses into senseless mental slumber nor technologically deterministic assumptions about the inherently impoverishing role of the mass media as opposed to literacy and direct orality (of the kind suggested in Neil Postman's *Amusing Ourselves To Death*) need be invoked to explain what has happened.[3] Without attributing sinister motives to the forces which have promoted this process, the first and most important point to

3.   N Postman, *Amusing Ourselves To Death*, London, 1986.

recognise is that postwar Britain has seen an appropriation of mass discussion by remote and unaccountable media agencies, and coextensive with this has been an etiolation of autonomous discussion which has been unmistakably disempowering. Whether this process is explained within the context of Chomsky's claim that the ruling elite needs to 'engineer consent' by means of the mass 'manufacturing of illusions',[4] or Herbert Schiller's claim that 'information inequality' is the inevitable price for 'the corporate takeover of free speech',[5] is a question separable from the observation that this process has occurred, and that it has been highly enervating to a civic culture which purports to be democratic. It remains to consider examples of this historical development, concentrating on the mass media's usurpation of electoral debate; of continuing discussion as channelled through electronic forms as diverse as *The Brains Trust* and radio phone-in programmes; and of the ultimately individualised and narcissistic verbal public witnessing embodied in TV 'audience discussion' shows such as that made popular by Oprah Winfrey.

When, at the beginning of the British general election of 1987, the television interviewer Brian Walden observed that no leader would come to power without first being exposed to public scrutiny on his well-respected Sunday afternoon programme, a significant comment about the condition of British electoral democracy was being stated. Of no small significance was the source of the comment: an ex-Labour MP, who as an elected backbencher could hope to have no comparable powers of making and unmaking national leaderships. Now as an unelected and unaccountable mass-media pundit, imbued with a claim to balanced neutrality, he could openly profess such power. What was being said by Walden, quite rightly and without intended arrogance, was that British elections cannot be won by those not invited to appear on television. This is TV in its most explicitly mediating role: literally presenting to the electors those wishing to be elected who are thought worthy of public scrutiny. The election becomes a matter of mediated rather than free choices. Whereas the legal freedom to stand in an election is determined by money (the price of a deposit) and minimal support, at least for the freedom to stand as a candidate (the requirement for a small list of official nominations to

4. ES Herman and N Chomsky, *Manufacturing Consent: The Political Economy of the Mass Media*, London, 1988.
5. HI Schiller, *Information Inequality: The Deepening Social Crisis in America*, London, 1996.

be submitted to the Returning Officer), the principle of mediated choice is determined neither by money nor paper support (as was seen at the launch of the ultimately abortive Social Democratic Party), but by media decisions as to suitability for presentation. Surprisingly little research has been conducted into how such suitability is judged, not least because much of it is implicit, informal and encoded in media terminology relating to 'balance' and 'effective presentation' which is rarely susceptible to honest investigation. Rather more has been written about the effect of televisual mediation upon politics; we do know that how people vote has become increasingly related to what they see on television. If 1987 represented the nadir for the three main contenders for political leadership, the 1992 election showed no remarkable improvements. It was in the latter election that a televisually unappealing leader seemed to defy the trend and achieve victory despite his media reputation as a bore, the eccentric appropriation by means of 'soapbox communication' in a gimmicky simulation of traditionally unmediated communication. Perhaps Major's publicity team recognised that the Walden principle had gone too far and it was time to appear to get back to the basics of democratic discussion; more likely, the controlled moments of soapbox theatre were an attempt to represent Major as a simple man of the people (his own selected people were recruited to surround his soapbox, it should be noted), and thus save him from the ravages of ferocious media interviewers.

Despite the contrived nature of Mr Major and his soapbox, his use of this medium was indeed a return to a form of democratic communication which had once been important, and often decisive, in electoral contests. Just as many early open-air meetings took place in opposition to legal convention at gatherings to nominate candidates to become MPs (see Chapter One), so it was the case that selected candidates increasingly made use of the public platform as a direct way of attracting votes. After the two major extensions of the franchise to working class men, in 1867 and 1884, no politician facing a contested election could afford not to speak to his (or her) electors directly. The hiring of halls for this purpose was an essential part of all election campaigns from the 1880s to the 1960s. (Most parties organise at least one constituency rally or speechmaking event of their own even today, but these have come to be regarded less a means of communicating with undecided voters than of providing rhetorical whiskey for the committed troops.) Even when indoor public meetings were a real part of the democratic culture, most political organisers realised that the widest direct impact upon local voters could be achieved by open-air street and park meetings where genuinely undecided and often indifferent potential voters could be involved in discussion, at least on the level of entertainment. We have seen in the diverse novels of Eliot, Tressell and Spring that this almost saturnalian encounter between the would-be leaders and the crowd was a necessary and much-enjoyed part of the modern British electoral tradition. Those of the political elite were compelled to abase themselves temporarily before those whose votes would determine the rise and fall of political ambitions and careers, even though the ambitious and the careerist would ordinarily have no reason to address such people except as servants or hired hands. The growth in importance of the public platform in elections led to a change of political language. Ideas had to be made more accessible. The contempt associated with the third person plural gave way to a professed amiability as the second person plural could not be avoided, and then a contrived togetherness as the first person plural was attempted. Of course, after the election the crowd could become 'they' once more, but without doubt it was the need to address directly this 'they' which led to a virtual disappearance of many of the excesses of contempt for the crowd (the mob, the rabble, the scum) which had characterised so much mid-Victorian political rhetoric.

It was in response to the Turkish atrocities committed against the Bulgarians, and the rise of popular feeling against government indifference, that politicians pursued an unprecedented campaign of direct address to the people via the public platform. *The Daily News*, on 6 September 1876, noted that 'the large public meetings that are now being held all over the country' represented a powerful 'movement of public opinion determined to assert its rights against those who were misrepresenting it', that is, parliament. Speaking to an open-air meeting of 10 000 listeners at Blackheath, Gladstone, whose contempt for the workers assembled in Hyde Park two decades earlier we might recall, stated:

'I have lived long in public life, I have witnessed many vivid movements of the popular mind, but never one to compare with that which, during the last fortnight, has taken its commencement, and has swollen with such immense rapidity... to the dimensions of a national movement... it has been a popular movement in contradistinction to an autocratic movement... the working men in the first instance raised this flag under which we are now marching.'[6]

6. *The Times*, 11 September 1876.

In 1879 the same Gladstone embarked upon his Midlothian campaign; arguably, the first modern electoral activity since the coming of the popular vote. In it Gladstone appealed directly to those whose votes his party sought, making it impossible thereafter for politicians to seek support without paying their respect to the voters in such platform campaigns.

By the early years of the twentieth century it was the case that most people's principal encounter with parties soliciting their votes at election time occurred at public meetings. In the 1920s areas like Hastings and Woolwich had continuously-running outdoor platforms at which daily attempts were made to win over floating voters. Of course, the press, which was deeply partisan, was already having an impact upon voting intentions by this time, but what was most remarkable was the remaining power of locally-experienced discussion to determine public opinion which remained invulnerable to imposed manipulation from nationally-organised opinion formers.

In the 1945 election campaign, which was in so many ways the most important of this century, the party leaders followed the tradition of Gladstone in touring the country and speaking to the voters directly. (The Conservative leaders embarked on fewer of these speaking tours, and perhaps this partly explains why they lost.) But in this election a new factor diminished attendances at meetings and set the pattern for a longer-term change; this is noted by McCallum and Readman in their pioneering electoral study:

'The chief explanation for the quietness of the election and the comparatively thin attendance at meetings was undoubtedly the influence of the [BBC radio] broadcasts. These were listened to by a surprisingly large part of the population. The BBC estimated that the average audience for each of these broadcasts was 44.9 per cent of the adult population... This is a complete answer to the question why attendance at meetings tended to be small, since it gives an alibi for nearly one out of every two members of the adult population during the time in the evening in which election meetings were generally held. It would seem to give the lie to suggestions that the electors were apathetic, since much interest and concentration were required of the elector if he were to sit through, and listen intelligently to, 20 minutes of political argument from an unseen voice, often of dull delivery.'[7]

7.   RB McCallum, *The British General Election of 1945*, London, 1945, p94.

This requirement of having 'to sit through and listen intelligently' placed the potential voters in a role of passivity and expected subordination to the speaker's standards of political intelligence, which marks a crucial erosion of interactive dialogue.

In the next general election, in 1950, the decline of public meetings and the sobriety of these 'instructional' events was noted by observers. In *The British General Election of 1950* HG Nichols noted: 'For the liveliest rallies between the hecklers and the heckled one had to go to the larger halls or the open air.' Despite the election being held in February, the weather was milder than usual at that time of the year, and, Nichols notes, 'their employment... was... more widespread than had been expected'.[8] They survived, but were becoming increasingly less significant as more and more people turned to their radios to find out what the politicians were saying. Sometimes electors would be swayed by election broadcasts in which they could assess, though not question, what the politicians said; but often they were influenced by the radio reports telling them what the politicians had said.

A key moment in this process of electoral mediation was the 1959 election. Whereas in the previous election, in 1955, a majority of the population listened to radio whilst 62 per cent had no televisions, by 1959 over three-quarters of the electors had television sets in their homes. Before 1959 the BBC observed a self-imposed rule of not covering election campaigns for fear of being controversial. In 1957 the newly-established ITV broke the rule by covering the Rochdale by-election. In 1959 both the BBC and ITV covered the general election for the first time ever. David Butler, the eminent electoral analyst, regarded 1959 as having 'the first TV election'.[9] Street corner meetings were still held, but were less relevant to most people's voting intentions than the debates and messages created by the television station. Unprecedented expenditure on pre-election opinion-forming advertising was embarked upon by the Conservative Party, probably unrepeated on such a scale until 1979. According to Treneman and McQuail's innovative study of the effects of TV in the 1959 election, only 15 per cent of voters polled 'claimed to have seen their candidate somewhere during the campaign, less than half this number at open-air meetings'.[10] A larger proportion of polled voters saw their candidate on a single ITV *Election Marathon* programme than at outdoor

8.   HG Nichols, *The British General Election of 1950*, London, 1951, p94.
9.   D Butler and R Rose, *The British General Election of 1959*, London, 1960, p17.
10. J Treneman and D McQuail, *Television and the Political Image: A Study of the Impact of Television on the 1959 General Election*, London, 1961, p103.

meetings. This simply could not have been the case at any previous election. The *BBC News* showed speakers addressing open-air meetings on two occasions during their three-week election coverage. We can assume from this that such images were still recognisable – and perhaps even comforting to those seeking reminders of a living democratic culture – although it is something of an irony that the best hope of an open-air speaker to be noticed by a major audience was via the very medium which was diminishing the size of the traditional audience.

BBC radio increased its output of *Any Questions* programmes during the 1959 campaign. Perhaps this was an attempt by radio to compete for an audience with television; certainly it was a form which relied more than TV on the imagery of uncontrolled discussion of the kind known to occur at real public meetings. But these were not real public discussions; the platform belonged to those empowered by the microphone, and the role of the audience was to submit brief questions and then applaud with remote politeness. The same was supposed to apply to *The Last Debate*, a major attempt by Granada TV to bring the cut-and-thrust of election debate into the houses of the viewing voters. Leading members of the three main political parties were invited to answer questions from the audience, but the programme proceeded in a direction less rigidly organised and safe than most earlier BBC question and answer formats had invariably been. As Treneman and McQuail note: 'For some reason, perhaps because of the size of the audience, or the form of seating as in a galleried public meeting, or the absence of preparatory briefing, the audience interrupted and heckled on such a scale that at times the speakers were shouting to make themselves heard, but the outcome was a lively and memorable broadcast.'[11]

More than one in five local voters saw this broadcast. The uncontrolled moments in the Granada programme were regarded as problematical and to be avoided in the future. A rare repeat of this kind of 'audience takeover' of an election discussion programme was broadcast by London's Capital Radio on the eve of the 1979 general election; so robust was the audience and so persistent was at least one of the hecklers that the politicians more than once appeared to be mere straight men in a comedy routine.

Interestingly, the emergence of televised political debate was perceived at the time to be a means of injecting dignity and rational standards into public discussion; both of these qualities were presumed to be lacking

11. Ibid, p69.

from and alien to live public meetings. So, when McCallum and Readman noted their observations regarding the decline of meetings in the 1945 election, they could not resist the conclusion:

'... this method of radio campaigning has revolutionised the nature of British elections. It is bound to shift interest from the local fight to national issues, and from the local candidate to the leading champions of the parties. It means that conditions under which the elector is persuaded, and the nature of this persuasion, will have undergone a subtle but profound change. Many of those factors which formerly tended to distract him from rational and critical thought are eliminated under the new method. The exposition of policy which is offered... tends to be more lucid and intellectually able than that delivered from the local platform. The elector is relieved from the physical discomforts inevitable in hot and crowded meeting rooms where seats are hard. But perhaps the most significant difference is that the element of mass emotion, which is always liable to arise and sweep through large congregations of people, intensifying their passions and clouding their judgement, is entirely absent.'[12]

Quite aside from the liberation from hard seats and collective passions offered by the mass media, the assertion is unmistakably stated that somehow there is a higher intellectual level attainable by the uninterrupted one-way speaker than that to be found in speakers in direct contact with questioning audiences. Treneman and McQuail pursued the same contrast between the mass media and the open-air platform:

'In television, a new quality had entered British elections. The party manifestos, which had once been shouted from public platforms by speakers well used to coping with hecklers, must now be directed to the family by the fireside. And the very people who would see no harm in a verbal scuffle at an open-air meeting or would rather enjoy reading in the newspaper about a boisterous exchange of views or a slashing attack on the policies of the other party, might bring a totally different set of expectations to what was being said through the screen in their own homes.'[13]

The shouted policies of the platform orator, satisfying the base expectations of a mob out for a scuffle, as against the cosy patriarchal imagery of

12. McCallum and Readman, op cit, p194.
13. Treneman and McQuail, op cit, p15.

dad, mum and the kiddies gathered round the televisual information box, left room for little doubt as to which was the more edifying process of political persuasion. After several decades of 'TV elections', the qualities brought to political discussion by television give rise to far less sanguine conclusions. Writing of American Presidential elections rather than British general elections, but with much applicability to the latter, Kathleen Hall Jamieson notes that in the 1940s half-hour speeches on commercial radio were purchased by candidates in order to convince potential electors; with the advent of television, half-hour speeches continued as the norm until 1952, shrinking to five minutes in length by 1956, and to 60 second political ads in the 1970s. By 1988 the average length of time that presidential candidates were heard speaking on the media during the Bush-Dukakis campaign was 9.8 seconds;[14] in the 1992 British election Martin Harrison was able to record that 'the average length of soundbite for the party leaders was down to about 18 seconds'.[15] One has to wonder whether, despite being freed from the cold winds and turbulent confrontations of open-air meetings, the hard seats and occasional demagogy of indoor election meetings, not to mention the obvious pressure involved in having to consider a political message for longer than it takes to consume a hamburger, is a price worth paying for the freedom to participate in free speech within a democratic culture in which serious thought by the audience is not seen as a disruption to the normal service of virtually senseless one-way communication.

So far have elections moved away from direct discussion that Dunleavy and Husbands, in their major analysis of the 1983 general election, did not even consider public meetings as a factor of persuasion in relation to voting intentions. Sixty-three per cent of voters polled stated that television was their most important source of political information – more than twice as many as those giving newspapers as their first source, and over 2000 per cent more than those giving any kind of personal contact as their principal source of information. Polls on public meeting attendance in 1979 found that 21 per cent surveyed had been to a political meeting, whilst in 1984-85 the figure fell to 8.6 per cent.[16]

Denver and Hands, discussing local constituency campaigning in the 1992 general election, note:

14. K Hall Jamieson, *Eloquence in an Electronic Age*, Oxford, 1988, p9.
15. M Harrison, 'Politics on the Air', in D Butler and D Kavanagh, *The British General Election of 1992*, London, 1992, p170.
16. P Dunleavy and C Husbands, *British Democracy at the Crossroads*, London, 1985, p95.

'It is generally assumed by commentators that over the past 20 years or so public election meetings have virtually disappeared... candidates and party organisers argue that this is simply an inefficient way of reaching the voters and the meetings waste the time of party workers who could be better occupied doing other things. It is certainly the case that in 1992 many candidates did not address public meetings. Amongst our respondents [election agents for the major parties in 144 constituencies], 31 per cent of Conservatives, 53 per cent of Labour and 43 per cent of Liberal Democrats reported holding no public meetings at all.'[17]

The mediated images which represent political discourse have come to serve as substitution for any actual interactive political discussion between electors and those seeking election. An increasing attention to personality profiles of leaders and packaged party imagery has made discussion of first principles and social values obsolete at election time. Margaret Scammell observes how the Conservative Party's Director of Publicity, Gordon Reece, broke new ground in the transformation from political communication to party-brand marketing in 1979: 'The Tories waged a deliberately short campaign, all-ticket rallies cut down the risk of hecklers, the leader's tour was designed for photo-opportunities, and openings for reporters' questions or for displays of protest kept to a minimum.' The Labour Party too, she notes, has 'thoroughly incorporated' into its campaigning strategy the same '"elimination of risk" approach'.[18] The BBC's political correspondent, Nicholas Jones, whose *Soundbites and Spin Doctors: How Politicians Manipulate the Media – And Vice Versa* offers a depressing picture of contemporary democratic culture, expresses concern as to 'how complex ideas or detailed expositions are to be put across in a media environment habituated to the relentless pursuit of the soundbite: with political discourse increasingly reduced to a battle of slogans, there is a real problem for anyone who wants or needs to hold the listener's attention for longer than a few seconds'.[19] The Walden principle has triumphed. As

17. G Denver and G Hands, 'Constitutional Campaigning', *Parliamentary Affairs*, Volume 45, no 4, October 1992, p534.
18. M Scammell, *Designer Politics: How Elections are Won*, London, 1995, p276. See also Bob Franklin's *Packaging Politics: Political Communication in Britain's Media Democracy* (London, 1994), and Dennis Kavanagh's *Election Campaigning: The New Marketing of Politics* (Oxford, 1995). These three books offer very useful accounts of the growth of what Keane calls 'media democracy', and should surely become key textbooks in relation to the explanation of postwar British politics.
19. N Jones, *Soundbites and Spin Doctors: How Politicians Manipulate the Media – and Vice Versa*, London, 1995, p51. This is the most perceptive and informative critical ac-

Michael Heseltine put it, in his plea to the media producers during the 1992 general election: 'We depend on you. There is no other way we can get over what we want to say.'[20] Perhaps the discussion initiated by street corner, park and market square speakers was often superficial, susceptible to rhetorical abuse, and liable occasionally to confuse politics with either abstract philosophy or vulgar showmanship, but at least it was open and unmediated. It depended upon people wanting to say something to 'get over' what they wanted to say, without unaccountable institutions of mediation deciding whether it was fit to be heard; its reception depended upon the live responses of those who took the time to think and to question.

Whether it is more harmful for society to have vigorous public discussion but votes only for a minority (as characterised the Chartist age) or universal franchise and severely atrophied outlets for autonomous social discussion (as characterises our own age) is open to question. Without doubt, neither situation can be deemed democratic. As the Christian-radical media theorist, Michael Traber, rightly observed: 'Over and above voting and party politics, democracy requires people who can make their wishes known in public and who participate in the debate about the type of society and political process they aspire to.'[21]

The emergence of 'The Radio Talk' as an offering from those empowered by the microphone to a silent audience, was not an extension of public talk, but a substitute for it. Radio, and later television, have not offered real discussion, but one-way conversations, with the role of the speaker and listener clearly separated. The BBC's first chairman, John Reith, was morally self-assured about the function of such one-way communication: 'There was to hand a mighty instrument to instruct and fashion public opinion; to banish ignorance and misery; to contribute richly and in many ways to the sum total of human well-being.'[22] But who would determine the content of output which would achieve such a lofty purpose? An uneasy tension was to develop between the licence-granting government and the independence of the BBC Governors, and this has persisted to the present, with increasing intervention of a third force: the investors in broadcasting, often euphemistically styled as

count in modern times to be written by a broadcasting insider.

20. Cited in Harrison, op cit, p164.

21. M Traber, *The Myth of the Information Revolution: Social and Ethical Implications of Communication Technology*, London, 1986, p94.

22. J Reith, *Into the Wind*, London, 1949, p103.

'market forces'. In whichever of these three areas of power final authority rested, the clear fact is that it did not rest with the consumers of broadcasting. Listeners (and later, viewers) were conceived from the start as essentially passive recipients. Never was this made clearer than in the Beveridge Report on Broadcasting of 1949, in which the division of the population into classified intellectual catchment areas was expressed with candour:

'The Home Service... is a carefully-balanced programme, designed to appeal to all classes, paying attention to culture at a level at which the ordinary listener can appreciate it; giving talks that will inform the whole democracy, rather than an already informed section... Flanking it on the one side is the Light Programme which is... to act as a great "catchment area" for those who look to broadcasting purely for relaxation and amusement... Having gained the attention and confidence of this broad base of listeners, it is the aim of the Light Programme to interest them in life and the world around them... Flanking the Home Service on the other side, the Third Programme is designed in general for the serious listener.'[23]

This represented a sociology of communication consumption, rather than participation. Regulation of what the consumers could hear was firm and is well documented: in the General Strike of 1926 the BBC ensured that 'the public' was informed by a voice independent of the strikers who constituted most of the listening public; in 1928 the BBC submitted to an ordinance requiring it to deny air time to 'controversial' subjects; the wartime Coalition government issued an edict, not removed until 1956, barring radio coverage of any political issue within 14 days of its being debated in parliament. Radio talks deemed offensive to the government could be the subject of threatening questions in parliament, and serious transgressions of political protocol have always been linked, if only in codified form, to the government's power to deny funding to the BBC.

The BBC's first Director of Talks, Charles Siepmann, was appointed at a time of serious unease within the Corporation about what might and might not be talked about on air. In 1933 Vernon Bartlett, the BBC's foreign correspondent, had given a talk which was regarded as being pro-German. Such an outcry was raised, in parliament and elsewhere, that Bartlett soon afterwards left the BBC (only to be elected to parliament

23. Cited in J Dunbar, *The Radio Talk*, London, 1954, p55.

five years later). In 1934 William Ferrie, speaking of working class conditions, threw aside his approved script, denounced the censorship of the BBC, and went on to give a live talk which the BBC was too embarrassed to stop. In 1937 a talk by John Hilton was deemed to be pro-Russian, and a decision was taken 'to keep off Communism and Nazism and Fascism for the next year or so'. As early as 1927 Hilda Matheson asked Reith for 'permission to experiment with one unwritten debate'. He replied that this would be acceptable 'provided you can be certain that things will not be said that will subsequently get us into trouble'.[24] Whilst all of this caution and self-censorship was going on, there were hundreds of street and park meetings taking place throughout the country at which all kinds of marginal views, unrehearsed debates and sharp conflicts of view were taking place which rarely led to any trouble. Why the extraordinary timidity on the part of broadcasters? The answer is surely that as soon as regulation and licensing is introduced into discussion, one enters upon a slippery path leading back to the uninterrupted sermons of a pre-Reformation clergy which was more prepared for the voice of the Messiah's second coming than the questioning whispers of congregants. So it was that the BBC Talks Department proceeded with such foolish series as the 1932 *Casual Conversations*, which were anything but casual as they were performed by actors reading scripts. A few prewar efforts at unscripted discussions involving questions from the audience were attempted, especially by the BBC Northern Region, and these proved very popular, despite the absence of omni-directional microphones which made it impossible for listeners to feel as if they were participating in a live debate.

By far the most important of the BBC's early attempts to guide public discussion was *The Brains Trust*, which first went on the air on 1 January 1941 with the title *Any Questions*. (This latter title, which was soon abandoned, was to be reused later for another long-running and highly-controlled radio discussion programme. It in turn spawned the popular BBC TV discussion programme *Question Time*.) *The Brains Trust* attracted an audience of 29.4 per cent of the listening public by 1945. But what were they listening to? The purpose of the programme was to present the discussion of ideas as a form of passive entertainment in which the questioning laity were divided functionally and spatially from the opinion-giving experts. Listeners could send in questions, but the freedom to answer rested with those chosen to sit behind the microphone. From Julian

24. Cited in A Briggs, *The History of Broadcasting in the UK*, Volume 1, London, 1961.

Huxley, CEM Joad, Malcolm Sargent and Barbara Ward came the priest-like voices of authorised public discussion of matters profound as well as trivial. Of the questions sent in to be discussed the politically sensitive were simply censored. For example, in February 1943 the BBC's Board of Governors decided that it would not be appropriate for a question about the desirability of the profit motive to be discussed on *The Brains Trust*. This was not an exceptional edict; for years before then questions regarded as likely to irritate the government were rejected for discussion. The official line of demanding caution in relation to political discussion was in marked contrast to the open-air tradition of banning no subject that people were prepared to speak about. The BBC's justification for its control over discussion, whilst contingently related to the question of wartime morale in a few cases, was more generally based upon the belief that the principal functions of broadcast discussion was to serve as an edifying service, and to offer entertainment. Needless to say, those doing the edifying were thought to be in a better position to determine the terms and scope of the debate than those who were to be edified. And the requirement of light-hearted entertainment allowed the programme's controllers to justify evasion of serious political themes or radical views on the grounds that these could be disruptive to such an end.

The Brains Trust symbolised the kind of paternalistic and somewhat condescending discussion which characterised the British media for the first quarter of a century of the BBC's existence. It helped to foster a cultural regard for ritualised and pompous expert contemplation, noted for its refined distance from the rhetorical devices of platform oratory and the spontaneous uncertainty of the speaker-crowd-heckler relationship. Uninterrupted, the experts could afford a calm self-assurance which arises directly from the knowledge that one's arguments face no immediate challenge. This was undoubtedly a step backwards as far as democratic discussion was concerned.

Both radio and television discussion has become less ritualised and controlled in recent years as the earlier regulations of 'public broadcasting' — in effect, broadcasting to and not *by* the public — have evolved into a greater multiplicity of mass media outlets, a weakening of legal constraints, experience of a greater variety of types of broadcast talk, and a thinning of the once obvious line between experts and lay people. The best example of a breakthrough in form and content in radio discussion has been the emergence of the phone-in programme.

Phone-ins came to British radio in the late 1960s. They had previously existed in the United States, Canada and Australia. In Britain their emergence coincided with the spread of local radio, at first run only by the BBC, but after 1974 by newly-legalised commercial stations as well. BBC Radio Nottingham ran the first phone-in show in 1968, hosted by Tony Church. (Before long BBC Radio London broadcast a daily phone-in show hosted by David Simmonds.) Listeners were at first unused to the concept of talking in their homes and being heard by others through their radios. The early phone-in producers had to teach people to find their public voices. In 1974 the London Broadcasting Company (LBC) was set up as the first local commercial talk station in Britain. It had a strong commitment to phone-in broadcasting, and, after a year, recruited from Capital Radio Brian Hayes, a pioneer of quality Australian radio phone-ins and probably the person who did more to establish a culture of phone-in discussion (in London, if not further afield) than anyone else. This is not the place to record the early history of British phone-ins and the significant role of Hayes and others.[25]

The key question raised by the phone-in concerns the extent to which it can be regarded as a forum for democratic discussion in the way that open-air public meetings once were. Can it be argued that these pro-grammes are an electronically sophisticated form of free public discussion which have superseded the essentially Victorian and Edwardian street and park gatherings? There are five factors which militate against radio phone-in programmes performing such a role. Firstly, although phone-ins tend to invite callers to discuss certain topics, or even to introduce topics for discussion within 'open line' formats, the medium does not afford callers the opportunity to move beyond the specificity of topical com-ment to the development of broader ideological or historical themes. For example, a radio phone-in discussion on whether Sinn Fein should be banned from the airwaves (itself, of course, a limitation of phone-ins which is less enforceable in public meetings) allows callers to state their views for or against such a ban, but will invariably rule out of order dis-cussion relating to 'root causes' of the matter, or of democratic theory. Such excursions into more analytical and sweeping political discussion are ruled out as being inappropriate. Partly, this relates to the second factor: phone-in programmes are limited by constraints of time. Each caller can only be allowed to speak for a few seconds at the outset, followed by a few minutes at the most of discussion with the presenter. The opening 'speech', even if uninterrupted for as long as a minute, is hardly sufficient

25. See my *Talk Radio and Democratic Culture* (Dartmouth, forthcoming) for an account of this much-neglected aspect of radio history as well as its contemporary political significance.

time to develop analytical discourse. Whereas 30 to 60 seconds of anecdotal, experiential speaking may be long enough to make a strong impression, any serious analyst of social affairs or rhetorician of social change is likely to appear foolishly generalised under the constraints of such compression.

Furthermore, once callers have opened in broad thematic terms, the presenter is entitled to push them into specific comments upon their own agenda of topics. So, in a discussion on the Sinn Fein ban, even if a caller managed to achieve the luxury of 60 seconds of broader analytical speech, this will almost certainly be followed by an attempt on the part of the presenter to divert the caller from the broader discussion of, let us say, the nature of state censorship within democratic societies, to particular issues relating to the ban in question. It is perfectly proper for presenters to do this. They see phone-ins as facilitating topical debate rather than broader thematic discussion. The latter, by the very nature of its rational demands, takes longer than the former, and is frequently deemed to be boring within the context of easy-listening radio.

Other time constraints interfere with the elaboration of analytical points: on commercial radio phone-ins breaks for advertising dictate the end of calls, and on all phone-ins breaks for the news or traffic reports interrupt the flow of sustained discussion. Callers are generally discouraged from becoming too regular, and callers who are seen to be 'one-tracked' are rejected. The right of the producer, or even the switchboard operator, to refuse a call constitutes a third major factor limiting the chance of phone-ins to become free and open discussions. Those involved in pre-broadcast call selection act as gatekeepers, stacking calls on the basis of what they think is interesting. Norma Ellen Verwey raises serious complaints about the BBC's 1974 *Election Call* phone-ins in which the impression of calls being broadcast on a first-come first-served basis was given, whereas calls were actually selected by the producer on the basis of what he thought would make for interesting discussion. Verwey contrasts this with certain Canadian local commercial radio phone-ins where no call selection took place.[26] In fact, most British phone-ins operate some degree of call selection.

There have been some BBC programmes where most calls are selected before the phone-in goes on the air, and there appears to be an attempt to select callers who will ask those questions which an interviewer would

---

26. NE Verwey, *Radio Call-ins and Covert Politics*, Aldershot, 1990, pp1-72. This deals with Canadian phone-ins.

have asked anyway. These conform to what Verwey rightly calls 'phoney phone-ins' in that the callers are effectively being used as surrogate BBC interviewers.[27] Most radio phone-ins in Britain are not so rigidly selective, but callers regarded as boring, ideologically preoccupied or mad will be refused admission to the phone-in discussion. Very often they will be told that their point has been noted, and they will be called if wanted for broadcast. Having overcome this hurdle of being selected by an unelected, unaccountable and usually anonymous gatekeeper, a fourth factor comes into play to inhibit democratic discussion: this is the enormous power of the phone-in presenter. This person can interrupt callers, cut them off in mid-flow, and even comment on their views after they have been cut off, so denying the caller any right of reply to responses which are sometimes based upon misunderstanding or distortion, and are occasionally offensive or even vicious.

There can surely be no other form of conversational discussion, apart from those involving perverse disparities of power roles, in which the two parties are communicating with so transparent an imbalance of rights. Professional phone-in presenters generally endeavour to allow callers to 'have their say', but any tendency on the part of the caller to deviate from the conventions of the format, to question the presenter's wisdom, or to refuse to follow the course of discussion demanded by the presenter will usually result in the use of the cut-off button. Indeed, callers have been cut off by some presenters for calling the presenter by the wrong name, for failing to hear or comprehend a comment made by the presenter, or, in the case of one popular London commercial radio presenter, for being regarded as 'an obvious loony' after having spoken for 10 seconds. Worse still is the right of the presenter to say anything, within the bounds of libel, about a caller after having cut him or her off. This is not only alien to democratic practice, but is highly unethical. A final factor limiting the democratic nature of phone-ins is the lack of interaction between callers. Occasional, and generally unsuccessful, attempts at enabling callers to speak to other callers have been tried, but these have been entirely mediated by producers who determine the length of any interaction, and select suitable cases for interaction on the basis of simplistic notions of oppositional views. Such interaction never constitutes sustained debate. Indeed, for the reasons given, radio phone-ins are antithetical to meaningful democratic discussion.

The essentially undemocratic nature of radio phone-ins has not

27. Ibid, p239.

stopped broadcasters from advertising them as the embodiment of a democratic public arena. For example, when LBC lost its franchise to broadcast in 1993, it persisted in playing promotional advertisements declaring itself to be 'The Voice of London'; in the almost hysterical campaign to save the station it was repeated frequently that the large phone-in component of its output was democracy in action. This was fraudulent nonsense, as was the LBC 'Talkback' jingle which regularly informed listeners that 'you don't need a soapbox to have your say when you call LBC' (thus promoting the illusion that calling a phone-in programme somehow affords citizens the same rights as was inherent in the soapbox tradition of uncontrolled free speech). On a national level, similar accusations of false claims as to phone-ins being 'the voice of the nation' can be levelled against Talk Radio UK, established as the nation's first national phone-in station in February 1995. Phone-ins often accentuate the gulf between the authoritative expert and the humbly questioning laity. In many cases discussion comes to resemble *The Brains Trust* with the only different feature being that now the great and the good consent to address directly the questioners whose brains they might be said to be holding in trust. On many phone-in programmes the star role of the presenter is in danger of overwhelming any attempt to achieve a multi-voiced discussion. This danger particularly perturbed Verwey, who noted that in the BBC's 1974 *Election Call* phone-ins the presenter, Robin Day, occupied 31.1 per cent of all the time spent in interaction.[28] In the USA, where the film *Talk Radio* was based on the murder of the phone-in presenter, Alan Berg, who specialised in insulting callers, there has been a recent growth in such abusive phone-in presentation, most notably in the case of the phenomenally successful Howard Stern. Profiled in the *Independent* on 14 May 1994, readers are informed:

'To pile insult on insult, Stern actually gets paid for spewing out this stream of invective, masturbatory reverie and scatology, and paid handsomely, too — $9 million a year... He owes both his fortune and his place in the competition for the governorship to the *Howard Stern Show*, a daily five-hour ramble through the murkier passages of his mind which originated through the New York FM station K-Rock and is syndicated throughout the United States to an audience of more than 10 million listeners...'

Stern's tendency to use callers as mere fodder for self-opinionated ranting

28. Ibid, p215.

and abuse of the vulnerable is occasionally imitated, with some English reserve so far, by British phone-in presenters who seem to have been seduced by the power of their position into regarding callers as expendable extras within the drama of the phone-in performance. All of this is a long way from Verwey's rather idealistic call for newly-appointed phone-in presenters to be 'humble, impartial and encouraging catalysts of casual call-in conversation'.[29]

The contrast between the democratic opportunities of autonomous public discussion of the kind associated with Speakers' Corner and the limited access to an audience offered by radio phone-ins is clear. The open-air speaker needs to pass no audition to address an audience. All that is required is a platform and a loud enough voice to attract passers-by. On a phone-in programme the would-be contributor to discussion must satisfy a member of the production team that what she or he has to say will be interesting. The open-air orator may speak for as long as is necessary to build an audience and develop a point of view. The phone-in contributor has a ready-made and larger audience than is to be found at most public meetings, but she or he is only at liberty to address it for a matter of seconds, making the development of a coherent or intelligent argument virtually impossible. At a public meeting the speaker is at the mercy of the crowd, which may question at any point and heckle ruthlessly. The right of the public speaker to dominate the proceedings is consensual: if the crowd is less than impressed by the oratory or the argument, it can take over the meeting. The phone-in contributor receives no feedback from the listening audience, unless a later contributor refers to what she or he has said. But, unlike at the public meeting, in the phone-in situation the speaker is at the mercy of a single presenter who may interrupt, deride, cut off the contribution in mid-flow, and even comment on what has been said after the speaker has rung off, often over-simplifying, distorting or being plainly offensive about what the contributor has had to say. At a public meeting the role of speaker and listener can interchange: members of the crowd can be invited to take the platform (a common way of testing the argument of persistent opponents at open-air meetings), or urged to set up a platform in opposition to the speaker. On phone-in programmes presenters retain the power of the microphone; callers who object to their treatment can hardly be advised to go and set up their own phone-in programme. Anyone with a serious argument to put before the public, seeking a democratic forum to state and debate his

29. Ibid, p219.

or her case, would be foolish to imagine that the phone-in programme provides such an outlet. Such programmes are deceptive insofar as they make claims to give the public a voice and to allow 'ordinary' people to influence one another. Indeed, on the question of influence, whereas there is considerable evidence that public meetings have played a traditional role of changing people's minds, such as in the 1945 general election, when relatively small and impoverished political organisations were able to influence substantial numbers of voters, the available evidence indicates that phone-in programmes produce no such effects. Verwey's research into listeners' reactions to the BBC's 1974 *Election Call* phone-ins (admittedly broadcast in the early days of British phone-in radio) showed that 91.3 per cent of listeners learned very little new about vital political issues by hearing these programmes, and less than 0.1 per cent of those surveyed changed their voting intentions as a result of what they heard.[30] The possibility of democratising the phone-in medium should not be dismissed, but, as they stand, compared with the kinds of public meetings now considered to be outmoded, these programmes represent a significant erosion of the culture of political democracy.

In what has now become a global village, it is television which has created the illusory market squares and street corners as pseudo-public places within which discussion can take place. Or, at least, what now passes for discussion in an age which has come to regard debate as consisting of fragmented anecdotes and soundbites, and in which 'the public' has been sociologised into an amorphous mass: one huge audience in a spectacle not of its making. Television is best at producing the representation of debate, with metaphorical sparks flying, recognisable names adopting predictable positions, and well-groomed audiences behaving like semi-conscious applause and laughter machines. Programmes like the BBC's *Question Time* are less a studio-based replication of the cut and thrust of the open-air meeting than a simulated gladiatorial combat in which members of the audience are principally performing a response function, either by cheering or booing the principal players, or by raising points from the principals' agendas.

Before turning to TV audience participation programmes and their functions as outlets for surrogate discussion, it is important to emphasise a well-known cultural tradition regarding television: it is not expected

30. Ibid, pp127-65.

that viewers sitting at home will believe sufficiently in the reality of television for them to talk back to it. To talk to one's television is generally considered to be a sign of madness. There is evidence that a number of people suffering senile dementia talk back to their TV sets, sometimes having quite sustained 'conversations' with newsreaders, soap opera characters and talk show hosts. Such pseudo-discussion probably brings a degree of comfort to the distressed. But it is deemed to be an insane condition. This link between madness and imagining oneself a part of the media pseudo-community is of recent origin; it has lasted for as long as radio and television producers have sought to convince people that they are part of such a community, and that it is somehow real. In the context of discussion, the same association between madness and the participating citizen exists, albeit to a lesser degree. As one listens to radio phone-ins, one encounters with some degree of embarrassment regular callers whose eccentricity is manifested mainly by their belief in the reality of the phone-in as a real community, the presenter as a friend, their few seconds of weekly public exposure as real communication, and the silent listeners as their neighbours. In fairness, there is more chance of these elements of interactive discussion being real rather than imagined for callers to phone-in programmes, as opposed to *The Archers* or *Coronation Street*, which also have considerable numbers of 'mad' people who attempt to initiate contacts with characters as if they were real. Nonetheless, the phone-in caller faces the stigma of being thought of as slightly crazy. Many give false names, and one has even encountered cases of callers refusing to indicate too much about themselves on air in case they are recognised and ridiculed. Appearance on a TV audience participation programme, whilst being nothing like as great a stigma as talking to the television set from one's armchair, is seen to be a rather pathetic role. One has not made it on to the box as a 'proper' guest, but as an anonymous, half-exposed, barely significant extra. For a professional person, seeking to create an image of articulate expertise, it could be disastrous to be seen as a face in the crowd on a TV audience participation programme, clamouring with the other audience members to compete for a few uninterrupted seconds at the microphone during which professional prestige and personal identity might just be salvaged. In the modern mass media, the crowd of the Le Bonist nightmare has been tamed and retained as props within an illusory representation of collective communicative interaction. This representation is seen by some media theorists as parasocial interaction. The main point about it, however, is that it is not real interaction.

On the matter of madness, one is not suggesting that standing on a platform in a park has always been regarded as a sign of sanity. Of course, the popular association between the open-air speaker and eccentricity or plain madness has existed, although it should be understood that this image is a relatively new one. (Even the medieval Fools were far from being perceived as madmen.) When outdoor oratory was a recognised communication tradition, practitioners were not regarded as peculiar characters. It has been with the decline of this tradition, the confinement of such oratory to specialised sites such as Speakers' Corner, and the emergence of the mass media as an alternative and more legitimate space for officially selected speakers to have their say, that the open-air orator has come increasingly to be seen as the oddball on a soapbox. But even within the context of such an image, there is no denying that public speaking is authentically interactive. Aside from some religious fanatics, whose often disengaged verbal testifying tends now to prevail at Speakers' Corner and other outdoor meeting sites, there can be no denying that open-air speakers are engaging in genuine social interaction. They may be derided for doing so, or seen as losers who cannot deliver their messages in any more prestigious forums, but one cannot say that they merely imagine that they are interacting with those who listen to and argue with them. The post-modern notion of parasocial interaction seems to rest upon the assumption that it does not matter whether real communication is occurring or not, as long as people imagine that it is. Senile dementia is in this sense a fashionably post-modern outlook.

The TV audience participation show (it is significant that it has become openly referred to as a show) is the contemporary substitute for the open-air meeting. Shows like the BBC's *Kilroy* and, the leading example of the genre, *The Oprah Winfrey Show*, imported from Chicago by both Channel Four and BBC2, invite audiences, both in the studio and at home, to gather round and speak their minds. The home audience is a silent presence in this public discussion, and the studio audience appears all too often to be performing a cathartic ritual of visible emotional release. Much of the discussion on these shows concerns collective responses of conscience to ethical dilemmas. Should a mother have had an affair with her daughter's boyfriend? The audience declares its verdict, almost in the fashion of a statistical print-out, with most people saying what most people at home would be likely to say, whilst a few outrage the consensus by stating what is then dismissed as manifestly wrong-headed. The sense of authenticity is brought to these studio discussions by two factors: the powerful weight of anecdotal testimony offered by audience participants, and the strong passions exhibited throughout the discussion. These are offset by the presence of 'experts' who have been invited to join the studio discussion. These people are the theorists. Their expertise lies in a detachment from anecdotally-based conclusions and generalisations based upon particular cases, and their ability to restrain their passions in the interest of rational thought and comment. They are respected for these qualities, and rightly so. The division is between the audience, all-feeling and little-knowing, and the theorists, who can enable the crowd to temper its prejudices and passions. The audience is expected to defer to the rational superiority of the experts, although occasional disdain for apparently abstract theorising is displayed, sometimes encouraged by pre-senters who are seen to perform a heroic role of saving the feeling mass from being overwhelmed by over-confident intellectuals. The discussion of ideas, and more so ideologies or idea-systems, is minimised in such studio discussions. Big theories tend to be ignored, or are stated by impli-cation, and theoretical dissent from the moral and political orthodoxies of the status quo are given short shrift.

Sonia Livingstone and Peter Lunt, in their major study of 'audience participation and public debate', raise some key questions about the po-tentiality for audience participation shows to provide a forum for real public discussion. First they ask: 'How far do the mass media provide a public sphere in which citizens may debate issues in a democratic fo-rum...?' Recognising that democracy cannot exist without the participa-tion of citizens in discussion, Livingstone and Lunt offer a sanguine view of the capacity of TV talk shows to provide such an opportunity: they 'argue that the media now constitute the major forum for political com-munication... Through diverse programme forms, including audience dis-cussion programmes, the mass media offer an informal, unofficial, but nonetheless large-scale, institutionally managed forum for public debate... audience discussion programmes can be understood as part of social space, as places where people congregate for public discussion, even as a "forum".'[31] This thesis, supported by interviews with participants in TV talk shows, and research based on focus group responses to selected shows, rests heavily on the notion of the active, critical citizen viewer who is able to utilise the elements of real discussion provided by these shows. It would be condescending to deny that viewers, no less than his-

31. S Livingstone and P Lunt, *Talk on Television: Audience Participation and Public Debate*, London, 1994, p10.

torians of communication or media theorists, can often discriminate between the anecdotal trivia and spectacular sentimentalism of these shows
and the moments of authentic debate. But, as in the case of radio phone-
ins, the problem is not so much one of making sense of what is there, as
recognising what has been lost historically by the adoption of this form
of discussion in place of other, more immediate (less mediated) traditions
of popular discussion which were once customary.

After the Los Angeles city riots in 1993, *The Oprah Winfrey Show* staged
a special studio discussion based in the city involving people from several
angles of experiential involvement. It was powerful TV, and it conveyed
an enormous sense of the frustrations, misunderstandings, fears and fading hopes of those who were in and around the riots. Koreans shouted at
African-Americans who shouted at white liberals who shouted at white
bigots. The participating audience shouted at the audience at home.
Oprah Winfrey shouted at the shouters, expressing the despair and bewil-
derment of many Americans – and, no doubt, the show's British viewing
audience of between one and two million. This show, like some others of
its type which have attempted to discuss controversial topical issues, was
characterised by a rawness of feeling untypical of the television medium,
and strangely close to the spirit of an open-air meeting in its spontaneity
and combative debating style. And yet it was a staged and ultimately controlled occasion. Like the debates held in Yale University in 1813-14, in
which each discussion closed with a pronouncement by Timothy Dwight,
the president of the college, as to the 'correct' conclusion to be drawn
from the debate, presiding over it was Oprah Winfrey, supported by her
privately-employed television production team. Her role was to ensure,
for the sake of 'good TV', that no person spoke for too long (more than a
minute, in fact); that anecdotal testimony did not transform itself into
ideological preaching; that 'moderation' (that euphemistic deceit of orthodoxy) never succumbed to the passions of 'extremist' analysis. The
objective was tolerant consensus rather than authentic discussion; the
quest for a comforting consensus served ultimately to deny the clash of
ideas in which true discussion consists. And consensual truth, here as in
all such shows, was implied to be embodied in the form of the presenter.
That was *The Oprah Winfrey Show* at its best. At its more usual level, the
show embraces a culture of neutered democracy in which an atmosphere
of complacent moral agreement, albeit based upon transparently fragile
ethical premises, creates an illusion that nobody needs to make a case for
any point of view because any point of view worth making is known. If

the open-air meeting was the free market in ideas, with speakers laying out their sometimes exotic or eccentric intellectual wares, the audience participation TV show resembles a run-down suburban supermarket in which the goods are placed on the usual shelves for predictable consumption, with only the presence of an occasional shoplifter to arouse chatter in the aisles and affirmation of the company ethos. Writing of the show in *The Guardian* on 20 July 1993, Angela Johnson suggested: 'Talk shows – like soap operas before them – act as surrogates for reality... Oprah's philosophy lies in the superficial quality of her curiosity. Viewers are encouraged to believe they are actually doing something, whereas in fact they are cocooned in their passivity.' In short, this is the embodiment of what Habermas calls a culture-consuming rather than a culture-debating society. It makes for entertaining television, but has little to do with public, democratic discussion.

The American phenomenon of seemingly ceaseless talk, here as therapy, there as freak-show entertainment, and every so often as simulated town meeting in which national soul-searching can be conducted as if it were lively debate, has given rise to what Howard Kurtz refers to as an elite of talk show presenters – 'the high priests of talk' – who 'wield unprecedented power, reaching millions with their daily gabfests':

'Whilst commentators in the age of Walter Lippmann or James Reston sought mainly to influence the governing elite, the new talkmeisters play to the masses. Presidents and prime ministers and putative leaders rush to appear on their programmes because the hosts are presumed to be in touch with the public... Yet the range of "debate" that unfolds on most television programmes is almost laughably narrow. Few panellists challenge the underlying assumptions of official Washington; any argument that lacks significant support in Congress is blown off the radar screens as irrelevant... Many of those who yak for a living exist in a hermetically sealed cocoon, rubbing shoulders only with other affluent insiders and leaving town only to speak to paying audiences.'[32]

Livingstone and Lunt, concentrating in their study on the rather more anodyne British talk TV shows, suggest: 'It is inconceivable that the meetings we see daily on audience discussion programmes would have occurred spontaneously during the course of unmediated social interaction.'[33] This is a curious observation. Unless it is suggesting that the spe-

32. H Kurtz, *Hot Air: All Talk All The Time*, New York, 1996, p10.
33. Livingstone and Lunt, op cit, p170.

cific order of the studio discussion, with its compressed time factors, its dominant presenter and its emphasis upon a single topic would only be likely to emanate from a studio discussion programme, it simply overlooks the reality of much wider and deeper social interaction which has existed within the tradition of autonomous public communication. The BBC's *Kilroy* show has brought people together for a hurried, staged discussion about the reintroduction of hanging. For many years visitors to Speakers' Corner in London could listen to the father of Hanratty, who had been condemned to death by a British court, and hear an eloquent case against state executions. They could argue with the speaker and with each other. Sometimes the discussion would continue into the darkness of the late evening. In the audience were men and women, old and young, those for whom prison life had been a reality, and those who had never so much as received a parking ticket. As they listened, debated and contemplated, there were other meetings discussing other subjects. To walk the few yards from the hanging discussion to the Catholic Evidence League, where atheists persisted in calling for a literal defence of the first chapter of Genesis, and then on to Ogilvy's platform, where the speaker's sardonic Scottish wit was unleashed upon a variety of 'good causes' from vegetarianism to the nuclear family, one had to be prepared to walk upon a remarkably uneven terrain. The common factor, whichever meeting one entered, was of discussion relentless and unchecked. On talk TV shows, the cultural geography is characterised by the dull flatness of the terrain: wherever you wander, from battered husbands on Monday to UFOs on Thursday, the main impression left is that the discussion will all be over when the producer waves his hand and the theme music begins.

Contemporary Silences: The Precarious Future of the Democratic Domain

A N EERIE silence pervades the contemporary public sphere. It is not that people are talking less – technology permits talk to spread further, crossing time zones and storing speech on machines in which communications can go on forever without people ever meeting or even thinking about the same subject at the same time – but there is a popular feeling that whatever one says is unlikely to have much of an impact upon a world in which everything has been said by experts, media pundits and prophetic pollsters who predict what people would say if they were asked to make real decisions. It is a paradox of a sophisticated liberal democracy that one of the most common expressions of political realism – in the workplace, down the pub, at the dinner table and before the TV screen – is to assume that talking is pointless, for it leads nowhere. As Blackwell and Seabrook have observed in a superb study of the collapse of contemporary hope, there is a 'conclusive finality' in which so much contemporary hopelessness and cynicism is rooted:

'It is a negative solidarity, a shared denial of the collective. In our isolation we are all the same. Up and down the country the same responses are heard, whatever evil confronts us. What can you do about it? If people are forced to seek a living rummaging through mounds of rubbish, if children are walking the streets of the cities for the purposes of prostitution, if people are frightened to give up their jobs in sweatshops redolent of Victorian England, if parts of London at night have the aspect of a vast funeral, few people will be found ready to declare that these things are evidence of a good or just society. Rather they say: "It's not right", "It's shameful", "It's disgusting", "It never ought to happen", "These things are a blight on civilised society", "It's unbelievable", "I never thought I'd live to see the day", "It makes you wonder what this country's coming to." But these conversations always end with a question that has become a kind of universal last word on everything: *"But what can you do about it?"* This is perhaps the most widely heard interrogative of despair in Britain today.'[1]

The recognition that such muttered impotence is quite incompatible with the enlightened aspirations of a self-proclaimed democracy is hardly acknowledged. The assumption is that Democracy is all very well, and certainly preferable to Dictatorship, but that the absence of a democratic culture in which anybody can at least begin to do something about anything must be taken for granted. Democracy is something one is told about on the TV News, a national treasure rather than a functional asset allowing people themselves to put wrongs right. Elected politicians are accused of being self-inflated gasbags, and parliament a mere talking shop. Never before have the elected been so distrusted by the electors; whilst a simultaneous mistrust of themselves has resulted in an epic silence on the part of millions of people: virtually a collective, tacit political sulk in the face of impotence and complexities beyond their reach. It is the age of global technocratic discourse; it is the epoch in which virtual silence extinguishes the vivacity of live public discussion.

Writing the history of silence as an intellectual and social trend is no easy task. What is there to say about silence which cannot be said on a sign on a public library wall? What can one say of the so-called silent majority which they refuse to say for themselves? When Peter Hall first directed the plays of Harold Pinter, the playwright who has best captured the repressive and oppressive silence of modern urban domesticity, he reportedly ran 'pause and silence' rehearsals to ensure that the actors understood that those moments when nobody had anything left to say were as dramatically significant as those when they came to speak, often with seemingly banal inconsequence.

Western culture has come to identify silence with dignity. At the most profound level of discourse concerning justice, often involving issues of life and death, the phrase 'Silence in Court' is the most authoritative command from personified dignity to the judged. Before voting citizens (subjects, to be accurate) enter the Strangers' Gallery to observe the workings of parliamentary democracy, they are required by law to swear a written oath that they will remain totally silent, desisting from speech even if the debaters in the chamber are presenting provable misinforma-

---

1. T Blackwell and J Seabrook, *The Politics of Hope: Britain at the End of the Twentieth Century*, London, 1988, pp39-40.

tion, or are speaking disparagingly about the viewing 'strangers' who elected them. Before international football matches the ritual of silence for the national anthem is occasionally broken by irreverent chants, but generally adhered to as a mark of respect, as if silence is a token charge to be paid by the public before the luxury of 90 minutes of relatively unrestrained verbal participation. Political meetings are increasingly now silent, visual events in which unprompted comment will spoil the running order of carefully-timed, TV-targeted stage acts. Not so long ago Harold Wilson or Quinten Hogg would challenge what were anticipated moments of well-aimed heckling (the former with wit, the latter with pompous indignation), but at least it was accepted, even at the highest levels of electoral debate, that the spontaneity of public comment was integral to democratic political discourse. These days the untamed heckler would be seen as an interference in a theatrical spectacle. Rather like the man watching a Shakespeare tragedy who insists on shouting out to Banquo, 'He's behind you!', a heckler at a political meeting would be asked to leave the hall, leaving the TV director irritated at the editing which such casual disrespect for the silent role of the audience will have caused, and the senior politician perched on his make-believe soapbox awkward in the presence of somebody taking the act for reality. (Efficient stage management ensured that this never actually happened to John Major during his electoral soapbox performances.)

Silent politics can be seen to reflect, at least to some extent, a contemporary dislocation of the civic environment, wherein more and more areas are becoming what urban geographers call 'dead space': places in which nothing in particular is supposed to happen, and from which spontaneous civic intercourse is unwanted or even forbidden. Richard Sennett's perceptive observation that 'were modern architects asked to design spaces that better promote democracy, they would lay down their pens'[2] is reflected in the city landscape by a profound insensitivity towards the need for any kind of lived democracy: any places where democratic citizens may gather and discuss. Sicilian Avenue in Bloomsbury, for example, is a delightful simulacrum of an open access pedestrian street, with its café tables along the side and its second-hand bookshop windows seductive to the eyes of contemplative browsers. How meanly and miserably this pleasant fabrication is spoilt by the small sign fixed to one of the artificial Sicilian pillars which reads: '*This avenue is private property and is not dedicated to the public. The public are therefore not entitled to use it as of right.*'

2.   R Sennett, *The Conscience of the Eye*, London, 1990, p xi.

Nearby there is Brunswick Square, now converted into privatised space as the Brunswick Centre. Sennett explores the nature of this dead space:

'The real lesson of Brunswick Centre is contained in its central concourse. Here there are few shops and vast areas of empty space. Here is an area to pass through, not to use; to sit on one of the few concrete benches in the concourse for any length of time is to become profoundly uncomfortable, as though one were on exhibit in a vast empty hall. The "public" concourse of the Centre is in fact shielded from the main contiguous Bloomsbury streets by two immense ramps with fences edging them; the concourse itself is raised several feet above street level. Everything has been done to isolate the public area of Brunswick Centre from accidental street incursion, or from simple strolling, just as the siting of the two apartment blocks effectively isolates those who inhabit them, from street, concourse and square.'[3]

In a recent election one of the candidates appeared in Brunswick Square, together with a handful of supporters, and attempted to hold an impromptu public meeting. Two things happened: most shoppers were shocked, and inhabitants of the surrounding flats peered nervously from their windows, not quite sure whether to dial 999 or turn up the sound on their televisions to drown out the intrusion of a human voice competing for their votes; then security was restored with the arrival of a guard whose purpose was to explain that election or no election this was private property and there could be no speaking in the empty square without written permission from the owners. (In the USA similar conflicts between the right of free speech, as guarded by the terms of the first amendment to the constitution, and the property rights of owners of privately-owned public places has resulted in several significant legal battles, including Robins v Pruneyard Shopping Center [1980], which upheld the right for private malls to be used as public places, and Shad Alliance v Smith Haven Mall [1985], which seems to have overturned the public function principle.)[4]

The romanticised reincarnation of the market square, with its suggestive connection to the ancient agora where discussion enjoyed a civic centrality, can often be deluding. Camillo Sitte's turn-of-the-century designs for a Viennese urban Gemeinschaft, with the creation of market squares in which people could randomly gather, was, as Carl Schorske has argued,

3. R Sennett, *The Fall of Public Man*, New York, 1992, p13.
4. See W Freedman, *Freedom of Speech on Private Property*, Westport, 1988.

incorporated culturally into the more utilitarian, embryonically Le Corbusierian world of modern Vienna.[5] In short, the image of an organic community is empty if there is no substance to the content of democratic life which it is meant to signify. Closer to home, and devised less romantically than Sitte's Viennese squares, there is the case of Milton Keynes. This is a 'New Town', designed to the measurements of artificial community which excited postwar Britain. During the privatising mania of Thatcherism, its town centre, like so many others, was privatised, leading to the bizarre decision to close the gates allowing the town's residents to cross the town centre at 11pm each night, thus leaving residents of each separated side of the town faced with a choice between a curfew, or a long detour to reach the other side. When the Chartists of Birmingham assembled in Chamberlain Square, or the unemployed of London in Trafalgar Square, they talked into the night, with torches and lanterns to let them see each other; only the threat of legal persecution could curtail the freedom of discussion. Today, no laws prevent the public from meeting, but the spaces in which literally open discussion can take place have been fenced off, guarded by private security firms. When the agricultural labourers in Doreen Wallace's *The Noble Savage* were denied use of the church hall, they had to meet in the village square; but where are their contemporary counterparts in free Milton Keynes supposed to go? The vivacity of the meetings held to support the striking miners in the 1980s and the Liverpool dockers in the 1990s, involving open and interactive discussion, often with female voices at the forefront, remind us that live democratic culture is not yet dead. These, however, are exceptions which defy the trend of these deafeningly silent times.

But was it not always so? Might one be accused of grand, romantic historical self-delusion in assuming that there was once a public sphere in which discussion was accessible and robust? The most sanguine claim for the historical reality of such a sphere is to be found in the writings of Jürgen Habermas, most notably in *The Structural Transformation of the Public Sphere*. According to this thesis, the condition within which a public domain of unchecked discourse emerged was the rise of capitalist market relations in place of the titular rigidities of the feudal court. Just as capitalism opened the market to all, as long as they could pay to enter, it created what one might call a free marketplace of ideas. This began with the organised traffic in news, firstly of a narrowly commercial sort, but then relating to wider political information and opinion. In Britain, the forum

5.   See C Schorske, *Fin-de-Siècle Vienna*, New York, 1981.

for the discussion of news and new thought was the network of coffee houses, of which there were estimated to be approximately 3000 by 1710. These meeting places became more than social spaces for good company and the consumption of coffee (which had only recently been imported into Britain), but a domain of unprecedentedly unregulated and inclusive open talk. Different coffee houses specialised in different themes for discussion. Of course, this was, as Habermas acknowledges, an essentially bourgeois public sphere which emerged in the late seventeenth and eighteenth centuries. Its 'public' was not the public as a whole, but the newly-empowered middle class who were not aristocratic and yet not too poor to be ignored. As this new public deliberated critically upon affairs of state, parliament found itself for the first time under the influence of a new social force: not the monarchy, the Church or foreign powers, but the people themselves. It was not only in the London coffee houses, but in the Parisian salons and elsewhere in Europe that this new public domain of discussion emerged. From the memoirs and accounts of *salonniérs* such as Mesdames d'Epinay, Necker and Geoffrin, it is clear that there was an authentic spontaneity and discursive freedom about these gatherings, even if this was mixed in with a degree of stylistic affectation. 'There was scarcely a great writer in the eighteenth century', states Habermas, 'who would not have first submitted his essential ideas for discussion before the academies and especially in the salons. The salon held the monopoly of first publication: a new work... had to legitimate itself first in this forum.'[6] So it was that the role of orality preceded literacy as a means of testing and arguing out ideas. Even in Britain, when the *Tatler* was established by Addison and Steele in 1709, its significance was as a prompt for coffee house and other public sphere discussions. It was in Britain that the political dimension of such discussion first emerged:

'A public sphere that functioned in the political realm arose first in Great Britain at the turn of the eighteenth century. Forces endeavouring to influence the decisions of state authority appealed to the critical public in order to legitimate demands before this forum... Why conflicts that were thus fought out by involving the public arose so much earlier in Great Britain than in other countries is a problem not yet resolved. A literary public sphere existed on the Continent too as an authority to which appeal could be made. There, however, it began to become politically viru-

6. J Habermas, *The Structural Transformation of the Public Sphere*, originally published 1962, English translation published London, 1989, p34.

lent only when, under the aegis of mercantilism, the capitalist mode of production had advanced to a stage reached in Great Britain after the Glorious Revolution.'[7]

One can question the empirical accuracy of Habermas' narrative. In fact, well before the Revolution of 1688, there is evidence of an embryonic public sphere which the state could not afford to ignore: the popular participation in religious debates during the English Reformation, and the intense, inclusive political discussions leading up to and during the Civil War are evidence that Habermas dates the rise of an influential post-feudal public sphere of discussion rather too late.

It was the emphasis upon the universal accessibility of the eighteenth-century public sphere which most impressed Habermas: 'everyone had to be able to participate':

'The public sphere of civil society stood or fell with the principle of universal access. A public sphere from which specific groups would be *eo ipso* excluded was less than merely incomplete: it was not a public sphere at all. Accordingly, the public that might be considered the subject of the bourgeois constitutional state viewed its sphere as a public one in this strict sense; in its deliberations it anticipated in principle that all human beings belonged to it.'[8]

The democratic implications of this claim by Habermas are highly significant, and are often overlooked. Even if the so-called bourgeois public sphere failed to draw in the voteless working class, its principle of political culture made it impossible to refuse recognition to the lower orders once they found their own voices. So, when Bentham, who was hardly a democrat, considered parliamentary debate, he saw it not as the preserve of a political elite, but as the generator of 'a habit of reason and discussion' which 'will penetrate all classes of society'. In relation to this Habermas quotes the perceptive observation of Marx:

'The parliamentary regime lives by discussion; how shall it forbid discussion?... The struggle of the orators on the platform evokes the struggle of the scribblers of the press; the debating club of the parliament is necessarily supplemented by debating clubs in the salons and the pothouses; the representatives, who constantly appeal to public opinion, give public opinion the right to speak its real mind in petitions. The parliamentary regime leaves everything to

7.   Ibid, p57.
8.   Ibid, p85.

141

the decision of majorities; how shall the great majorities outside parliament not want to decide? When you play the fiddle at the top of the state, what else is to be expected but that those down below dance?'[9]

The Habermasian thesis addresses not just the rise of the public sphere, but its degeneration and transformation. What Bentham entertained as a basis for cultivating mass rationality (an idea later refined by Arnold), and Marx saw as revolutionary-democratic grounds for hope, others were to see as a threat. The 'chattering classes' of the coffee houses were all in favour of public discussion as long as it in no way subverted the state's defence of commerce. By the 1670s, however, 'the coffee houses were considered seedbeds of political unrest', and the government was complaining about the tendency of people 'not only in coffee houses, but in other places and meetings, both public and private, to censure and defame the proceedings of the State, by speaking evil of things they understand not, and endeavouring to create and nourish an universal jealousie and dissatisfaction in the minds of all His Majesties good subjects'.[10] The response was for discussion to be increasingly consumerised. The task of critical reasoning and publicising political views fell increasingly to privately-accountable professionals. The tension between the universal access of the market and the paternalism of the commercial elite resulted in victory for the latter. This Habermas calls 'the refeudalisation of the public sphere': the transformation of a critically-discussing public into the receivers of publicity. So areas of social culture which had once been open and unmediated have become refeudalised and commodified:

'Put bluntly: you had to pay for books, theatre, concert and museum, but not for the conversation about what you had read, heard and seen, and what you might completely observe only through this conversation. Today the conversation itself is administered. Professional dialogues from the podium, panel discussions and round table shows — the rational debate of private people becomes one of the production numbers of the stars in radio and television, a saleable package ready for the box office... Critical debate arranged in this manner certainly fulfils important social-psychological functions, especially that of a tranquillising substitute for action; however, it increasingly loses its publicist function.'[11]

9. Ibid, p126.
10. Ibid, p59.
11. Ibid, p164.

This connects directly to the spatial privatisation of the public sphere. Almost as if he is writing of the demise of the street corner meeting, Habermas comments upon the changed 'function of streets and squares... due to the technical requirements of traffic flow', resulting in a cultural geography which 'does not afford a spatially protected private sphere, nor... free space for public contacts and communications which could bring private people together to form a public'.[12]

The public of contemporary politics is increasingly a statistical aggregate or invented mass which is drummed up for moments of semi-ritualised political activity, such as voting, marching, clapping or booing: 'The public sphere becomes the court before whose public prestige can be displayed — rather than in which public critical debate is carried on.'[13] Like refeudalised peasants, modern subjects are more used to fulfilling democratic obligations than engaging actively as deliberating citizens.

The non-deliberative inertia prevalent within avowedly democratic constitutional cultures has generated genuine anxieties about the implications for civic culture. This has led a number of thinkers to apply their minds to the reinvigoration of democratic activity, including discussion. The study by Barnes, Kaase, et al in 1979, *Political Action: Mass Participation in Five Western Democracies*, suggested that 'the "grass roots" of politics seem shrivelled and starved of the nourishment of participation by the citizens'.[14] Such deep concern and the thought that it has produced is more significant in the United States, where civic identity is collapsing most transparently, than in Britain, where the current malaise mainly takes the form of a popular disenchantment with institutionalised politics: parliament and MPs, government officials, remote European bodies, and conventional parties which appear to have abandoned themselves to imagery and opinion-shadowing rather than the generation of ideas or principles.

Here is not the place to address this wider question of the failure of democratic institutions to win respect from many, or even most, of those in whose name they claim to rule; critical books by Andrew Marr, Peter Hennessey and Simon Jenkins have ploughed these fields with considerable critical force, although there is a danger that such thinkers are addressing a wrongly-diagnosed malaise.[15] They have exposed what is rightly

12. Ibid, p158.
13. Ibid, p201.
14. S Barnes, M Kaase, et al, *Political Action: Mass Participation in Five Western Democracies*, London, 1979.
15. A Marr, *Ruling Britannia: The Failure and Future of British Democracy*, London, 1995;

referred to as 'the democratic deficit' in a top-down fashion, presuming disenchantment with the structure and exercise of state power to be the root of the contemporary democratic malady. The implicit assumption in this is that the erosion of popular democratic culture is a consequence of constitutional inadequacies. More likely, popular disenchantment with the political process stems from a justifiable belief on the part of many people that the institutions of public deliberation operate to their exclusion. Do people really believe that parliament is less democratic than it used to be? Manifestly it is not; it is now televised and commented upon with both insight and irreverence more widely than ever before; those wishing to do so can observe the robust standards of scrutiny available to Select Committees since the 1979 reforms, which have at least gone further than anything else this century to bring government to parliamentary account; the conduct of MPs both in and outside parliament tends towards a greater informality and personal accessibility than ever before; the power of organised lobbies (admittedly, weighted towards the rich and already powerful) is at an all-time peak; and, despite the valid observations about the pathetic inefficacy of most official political oratory, one would be hard-pressed to find much fault with the scrupulous attention to formal democratic procedures within the parliamentary process (at least, in the elected chamber).

This is not to paint a picture of a democratic regime in great health, even if it is doing rather well compared to other constitutional democracies, but to suggest that the fault lies not in the institutions which do reflect some sort of democratic choice and can be called to some kind of democratic account, but in the institutional absence of a domain of democratic activity beyond the enclosed chambers of state power. In short, even if parliament were tremendously good at being democratic, MPs consistently honest and articulate, and power wielded with dispassionate indifference to entrenched interests, democratic culture would still be in peril. The reason for this is well grasped by Andrew Adonis and Geoff Mulgan, who argue:

'... not only decision-making, but political debate more broadly, is dominated by political professionals. Politicians develop the themes, the language, the policies, project them through the national media and test them through polls with the public present as a largely passive observer of

P Hennessey, *The Hidden Wiring: Unearthing the British Constitution*, London, 1995; and S Jenkins, *Accountable to None: The Tory Nationalisation of Britain*, London, 1995.

a closed system. When public concerns burst through, demanding that politicians respond, this is usually seen as a crisis. The popular opinion upon which this regime draws both directly through elections, and indirectly through polls, is thus to a large extent an echo of its own voice.'[16]

Contemporary democratic theorists have increasingly come to express the view that democracies need citizens who do more than merely vote within the framework of agendas set by others, and echo slogans devised by agenda-setting elites. The more citizens learn to participate deliberatively, the more they are likely to become good democrats. Rather than defining democracy in terms of formal procedures, such as voting, the new democratic theorists contend that such 'rights' are only worthwhile if they are accompanied by a culture of fully accessible critical deliberation in which no individuals are denied the opportunity, and indeed the incentive, to articulate and test their ideas concerning matters of social interest to them. Giovanni Sartori, alongside Dahl and Bobbio probably the staunchest recent defender of liberal democratic theory, has contended that the existence of a public free to form its own opinions is 'the substantive and effective foundation' of democracy, being 'the element which gives substance and effect to popular sovereignty'.[17] In short, without the formation of public opinion within a relatively autonomous public sphere, claims by societies to be practising democracy are somewhat hollow. This valid recognition has led to a sense of democracy in crisis — of voting devoid of sovereign debate — and a search for the ruins of a once-existing democratic culture. For those following Verba and Almond's Civic Culture model, and for Kavanagh, who has revisited and revaluated it, the problem is to preserve a deferential political culture whilst letting citizens *feel* that they have decisive influence within it;[18] for Parry, Moyser and Day the issue of participation concerns the power of citizens to influence actively, though not necessarily to displace, political elites;[19] for Benjamin Barber the task is to redefine democracy, liberating it from its 'thin' liberal constraints, and creating 'strong' features which emphasise a participative impulse

16. A Adonis and G Mulgan, 'Back to Greece: The Scope for Direct Democracy', *Demos*, 3/1994, pp2-9.
17. G Sartori, *The Theory of Democracy Revisited*, New Jersey, 1987, p96.
18. GA Almond and S Verba, *The Civic Culture*, Princeton, 1963; D Kavanagh, 'Political Culture in Great Britain: The Decline of the Civic Culture' in GA Almond and S Verba (eds), *The Civic Culture Revisited*, London, 1989.
19. G Parry, G Moyser and N Day, *Political Participation and Democracy in Britain*, Cambridge, 1992.

towards the common good;[20] for Paul Hirst a 'post-Marxist' return to nineteenth-century associationism is the best hope;[21] John Burnheim argues for a further return, to the Athenian model of direct democracy;[22] James Fishkin has proposed and helped to implement the worthwhile idea of deliberative polling, participation in which encourages informed discussion amongst representative sample groups of the public whose deliberations offer a prescriptive, recommending force to their fellow citizens;[23] for Graeme Browning and a growing number of converts to the democratising potential of telematics, the largely anarchic subterrain of cyberspace offers a return route to a robustly democratic public sphere.[24] This latter model of participation has proved particularly seductive to the most recent crop of democratic theorists who entertain techno-utopian visions of global democratic discourse shooting its way down the information superhighway, allowing everyone (but for the majority of the world's inhabitants, who are technologically disenfranchised) to erect their own cyber-soapboxes, with interactive computer-anoraks becoming the principal participants in discussion, rather than dangerously assembled public gatherings.

Barber's utopian-democratic proposal for 'strong democracy' rests heavily upon the concept of 'strong democratic talk' involving 'listening as well as speaking, feeling as well as thinking, and acting as well as reflecting'. This appears to encourage a form of unmediated democratic discussion, but in reality, despite his protestations to the contrary, the strength of Barber's model is characterised by a strained rhetoric of ideological compromise in which 'talk is not used to chart distinctions in the usual analytical fashion, but to explore and create commonalities'. Is this not a plea to abandon the intense rigours of rational debate for the sake of political tranquillity? For Barber, 'healthy political talk' can be measured by 'the amount of silence it permits and encourages, for silence is the precious medium in which reflection is nurtured and empathy can grow. Without it, there is only the babble of raucous interests and insistent rights vying for the deaf ears of impatient adversaries.'[25] But surely

20. B Barber, *Strong Democracy: Participatory Politics for a New Age*, Berkeley, 1984.
21. P Hirst, *Associative Democracy: New Forms of Economic and Social Governance*, Cambridge, 1994.
22. J Burnheim, *Is Democracy Possible?*, Berkeley, 1985.
23. J Fishkin, *Democracy and Deliberation*, Yale, 1991; *The Voice of the People: Public Opinion and Democracy*, Yale, 1995.
24. G Browning, *Electronic Democracy: Using the Internet to Influence American Democracy*, Wilton CT, 1996.
25. Barber, op cit, p163.

the problem of the contemporary public sphere is that of too much silence (less reflective than tranquillised), and an insufficient 'babble' (if such a loaded term for a plurality of voices must be used) of competing views are in the air. To be sure, adversaries may well respond to rival articulations of interest or ideology with 'a deaf ear', but the point of democratic discourse is less to convert adversity into community than to permit the public to decide on the basis of clear argument which interest or ideology is most attractive to them. Barber's passion for empathetic listening and a ceaseless searching for mutuality suggests less 'strong democracy' than a weakened sphere for robust discussion.

For robust discussion to be encouraged, more respect must be accorded to what Ruth Finnegan describes as 'the relevance of speaking for social relationships and social culture'. She points out how amongst the Limba tribespeople words often possess an 'illocutionary force', meaning that they not merely suggest but constitute action in their utterance. This anthropological perspective serves as a useful rejoinder to those who make simplistic distinctions between 'mere talk' and 'real action'.[26] The expression and stimulation of thought is an act, not a prelude to an act. There is an intimate relationship between orality and the existence of a democratic public sphere, and it is a mistake made by more than a few historians (though not anthropologists) to assume that literate debate is somehow more cogent than that which is manifested in the transient form of speech. (Perhaps Bernard Crick's worthy and persuasive case for political literacy should embrace the need for better political orality.)[27] Edwards and Stenkewicz observe: 'In oral cultures words are at a premium. The Western literate distinction between "performance" and "ordinary conversation" is blurred by the wide range of different speech events, both formal and informal, which allow speakers to show off and enjoy their verbal skills.'[28] Ethel Albert, writing about Burundi speech behaviour, observes:

'Speech is explicitly recognised as an important instrument of social life; eloquence is one of the central values of the cultural worldview; and the way of life affords frequent opportunity for its exercise... Argument, debate and negotiation, as well as elaborate literary forms, are built into the

26. R Finnegan, 'Attitudes to Speech and Language Among the Limba of Sierra Leone', *Odu*, no 2, 1969, pp61-7.
27. B Crick, *In Defence of Politics*, Harmondsworth, 1982.
28. V Edwards and TJ Stenkewicz, *Oral Cultures Past and Present: Rappin' and Homer*, London, 1994, p15.

organisation of society as means of gaining one's ends, and as skills enjoyable in themselves.'[29]

This reverence for eloquence is important. Too often contemporary political observers equate persuasive oratory with empty rhetoric and demagogy. In a discussion organised by Channel Four before the 1997 general election to consider its plans for implementing a deliberative polling exercise, more than one political commentator present voiced concern about the influence upon such deliberation of 'good talkers', as if this were in itself a malignant or illegitimate basis for influencing opinion. The idea that political talk, be it related experientially, anecdotally or passionately, is inherently inferior to the coldly printed word or self-evident fact is a product of a political culture which has lost confidence in the most basic form of unmediated communication. In Malagasy culture, Elinor Keenan points out in her contribution to *Explorations in the Ethnology of Speaking*, orators are praised for their lack of brevity and circumlocutory skills. Contemporary interest in oratory is almost entirely devoted to speech which has been written down and then recited – the reverse of the situation perceived by Habermas in the salons and coffee houses where talk preceded literate formulations. So, Brian MacArthur's rather pedestrian *Penguin Book of Twentieth Century Speeches* includes almost exclusively pre-scripted rather than post-transcribed orations; Ludovic Kennedy's TV series, *The Gift of the Gab*, similarly emphasised 'great oratory' which was in reality the rhetorical delivery of pre-written speeches as opposed to spontaneous speech. It is as if speech only becomes respectable if it is first cleansed by literacy. Soundbite politics has increasingly become an ill-concealed deception based upon pre-scripted spontaneity; even informality must now be carefully rehearsed to maximise the impact of consumer satisfaction.

It is important, then, to recognise clearly the connection between the politics of language and the question of how some talk is legitimised, whilst some other is not. There are lessons here from the history of literacy, where 'proper English' was used not only as a medium of official propaganda, but as a pass of entry into legitimate public discourse. For Samuel Johnson, speaking of poetic expression, 'the most heroic sentiments will lose their efficacy, and the most splendid ideas drop their magnificence, if they are conveyed by words used commonly upon low

29. E Albert, '"Rhetoric", "Logic" and "Poetics" in Burundi Patterning of Speech Behaviour', *American Anthropologist*, Volume 66, no 6, part 2, 1964, p44.

and trivial occasions, debased by vulgar mouths, and contaminated by inelegant applications'. As Olivia Smith has so ably demonstrated, the late eighteenth-century battle between the rights of property and the liberty of the propertyless to express themselves resulted in an epic war of pamphlets between advocates of the status quo who sought, with condescension and frequent inaccuracies, to address 'the people' in their own language, while some middle class radicals, rather in the manner of contemporary student leftists, made strained efforts to adapt their communications to the language of the streets and factories.[30] So it was that the Association for Preserving Liberty and Property against Republicans and Levellers endeavoured, not least through the invented character of the gullible John Bull, to reflect in speech their own conception of the confused idiocy of the English working man, half prey to radical rhetoric, but ultimately saved by his innate sense of deference. The Association's radical opponents maintained a robust campaign of pamphleteering against the Burkean depiction of 'the swinish multitude' whose hoofs would allegedly tread down all learning. The radical polemicists failed ultimately to reflect the speech of those whom they spoke for but never as. This absence of colloquial language, with which the radical pamphleteers will have been familiar as members of the London Corresponding Society, pointed to a deeper embarrassment at the vulgarity and inferiority of working class orality.

The one exception to this tendency to silence the language actually spoken by workers is to be found in the writings of Thomas Spence. Himself a working class man, one of 14 children of semi-skilled Newcastle parents, Spence paid as much attention to the communication of his radical platform as he did to its content, even going so far as to devise his own phonetic alphabet. Declaring his aim 'to make the spoken language, as it ought to be, the archetype; of which the written language is only the type', Spence was perhaps the first urban thinker to resist theoretically and actively the claims of refined literacy over autonomous orality. Can it be coincidental that this interrogation of linguistic precedence was taking place at precisely the time when workers were first beginning to engage in organised rhetoric and discussion? The attempt to dismiss workers' speech because of the impropriety of its form has persisted to the present; Klaus Mueller considers what he sees as 'the arrested communication' of workers: 'the limited capacity of individuals and groups to engage in political communication because of the nature of their linguis-

---

30. O Smith, *The Politics of Language*, Oxford, 1986, p100.

tic environment (a restricted speech code) and not because of any apparent political intervention'.[31] Of course, Mueller accepts the social-environmental basis of such alleged limitations, but nonetheless the consequence of such theory is to relegate whole sections of society – perhaps the majority – to the role of silent spectators upon a political discourse which is possibly beyond their comprehension, and certainly too difficult to enter as verbal participants. The implication of such a claim for democratic theory is devastating, but one cannot help sensing that it is shared with increasing explicitness by political image-makers and campaigners for whom the eventuality of anything but a silent electorate has come to be regarded as almost a defiance of biological determinism. With very few exceptions, such as the experiments in democratic discussion conducted by William Gamson and his team in Boston, USA,[32] and the more recent exercises in deliberative polling inspired by the democratic theorist, James Fishkin, the equation between orality, vulgarity and ignorance has achieved the force of an implicit sociological truth.

The art of speaking and of organising democratic discussion has come to be regarded as a quaint anachronism. An exemplary illustration of the historical redundancy to which democratic forms can fall victim is JF Finn's manual from 1930, *The Outdoor Meeting: How To Organise, Conduct And Speak At It*. The appearance of such a book now would be inconceivable. Pulling the volume down from the further reaches of the bookshelves is to conduct a reality check that there was once a time when ordinary people needed to know how to organise, conduct and speak at open-air meetings. Nobody now needs these skills. Such meetings no longer take place (except when they are run by people who are old enough to have read Finn's manual, or by people who no longer know how to conduct or speak at such eccentric events). But, in the light of the condition for democracy outlined by Sartori, and repeated by most other political theorists, should not a political culture which celebrates freedom of public speech largely in the form of nostalgia or tourist spectacle be reconsidering its confidently-asserted claim to be a flourishing democracy? For Finn it was all so very clear:

'There is no doubt that it is necessary that more Members of Parliament of all parties should speak to the public out of doors, and also that more

---

31. K Mueller, *The Politics of Communication*, Oxford, 1973, p19.
32. WA Gamson, *Talking Politics*, Cambridge, 1992.

meetings should be held in the streets, parks and market places. The various extensions of the franchise have made the appeal to the masses more necessary than ever before.'[33]

Finn was a speaker for the then-thriving Anti-Socialist Union, an organisation only necessary because there were so many socialist orators to counter. The main problem for a modern 'anti-socialist' orator would be to have any idea of what grand vision it is that she or he might be expected to repudiate. Finn's delightful book contains 13 chapters, including 'The Chairman's Duties', 'Hecklers, Hostile Audiences and Questioners', 'Open-air Debates', and 'The Use of Sound Amplifying Instruments'; the latter are discouraged, not least because 'the use would be likely to lead to a breach of the peace if used by one organisation at a place where many meetings are usually held', and also 'those who gather in the open... are so accustomed to having at least some interruptions dealt with that they may be annoyed when ignored'.[34] Watching the BBC archives of recorded open-air meetings, there is a large slice of Tony Benn at Speakers' Corner in the 1980s reading from Peter Wright's *Spycatcher* as an act of public defiance against the government's banning of the book; Benn does not address the audience before him, but speaks with a microphone attached to his tie, media soundmen surround him, and he takes no questions from the hecklers in his audience, and clearly upsets nearby speakers who had come to deliver their messages unaided by 'sound-amplifying instruments'.

The descent of public speech into the realm of nostalgia is indicated by another virtually unnoticed disappearance: the manuals on how to speak and the vast number of speech anthologies which were published in abundance between the 1890s and the 1930s. These have been replaced by guides for PR and sales presentations (in which dexterity with the flip-chart and the VCR buttons far outweigh any ability to say anything of substance), and collections of quick-quotes which condense the oratory of a Martin Luther King or a Lloyd George to the equivalent of short riddles enclosed in Christmas crackers. Anthologies such as Fox-Davies' *The Book of Public Speaking*, Cochrane's *The Treasury of British Eloquence*, Wright's *Great Orations*, Adams' *Representative British Orations*, Paul's *Famous Speeches*, Jones' *Selected English Speeches*, and Bryant, Carroll, et al's *Historical Anthology of Select British Speeches* were not exercises in nostalgic recol-

---

33. JF Finn, *The Outdoor Meeting: How To Organise, Conduct And Speak At It*, London, 1930, p3.
34. Ibid, pp120-9.

lection, but reflections of a vivacious political culture in which well-devised speech was not a separate aspect of democracy looked after by 'communications experts', but an integral part of the democratic process. The very idea of a disjunction between the freedom to hold ideas and the opportunity to communicate them freely enervates and subverts democratic culture, converting pluralism from a sphere of actively discussed choices to a constitutional abstraction. This internal contradiction within many 'Actually Existing Democracies' causes justified anxiety to contemporary democratic theorists, such as Fishkin:

'Crucial voices may fail to achieve an effective hearing without the need to silence any of them. In a modern, technologically complex society, access to the mass media is a necessary condition for a voice to contribute to the national political debate. Unless the media permit the full range of views that have a significant following in the society to get access to the media on issues of intense interests to proponents of those view, then the full realisation of political equality has fallen short.'[35]

Danilo Zolo, discussing the Habermasian descent from public discussion to political publicity as narcotising spectacle, declares:

'... the political effects of mass communication are closely linked with the tendencies towards conformity, apathy and political "silence" which stem not so much from what is said as from what is unsaid, from what the communication filters tacitly exclude from the daily order of public attention. Silence is without doubt the most effective agent for subliminal persuasion in mass communication, and the most suitable instrument for a kind of negative homologisation of an information-based public. The political integration of information-based societies comes about far more through tacit reduction in the complexity of the topics of political communication than through any positive selection or discussion of them.

'Silence is not restricted solely to themes already formulated for inclusion on the political agenda. It also extends to the ability to conceive and express these themes in the first place. For, once they go beyond the bounds of the political code standardised by the media, political agents seem unable to form any proper outline of problems, to establish a clear conception of their own interests or to articulate them in a communica-

35. J Fishkin, *Democracy and Deliberation*, op cit, p33.

ble and socially effective manner. When they run out of stereotyped expressions, political consumers fall silent and become effectively dumb... Being swallowed up by "the spiral of silence" thus becomes a comforting alternative for those who dare not incur the risk of isolation posed by contravening mass media "public opinion". If they remain silent, they know that they can count on the complicity guaranteed by a political group to those who show that they share the prejudices and particularisms on which that group is founded.'[36]

Zolo points here to what is fashionably called 'agenda setting'. The unaccountable power to relegate public events and ideas to the margins or beyond the scope of the media agenda is a matter for democratic concern. But more dangerous still is a political culture in which whole outlooks are virtually silenced by media neglect or disdain, and in which dissident speakers are doomed to fend for themselves within a marginalised sphere of unrecognised and somewhat eccentrically autonomous unofficial communication.

Such isolation might be the fate of evangelical Christians or Muslims (both growing faster currently in Britain than the state church), or chauvinistic Europhobes, or libertarian socialists whose ideas fit neither labourist nor Leninist categories. In a truly 'free market of ideas' these outlooks could prosper or wither on the basis of critical public scrutiny. Faced with the paradox of legal freedom of expression alongside media repression by silence of views with no categorical place on the official agenda of outlooks worthy of serious representation, it is impossible to say anything of such views except that they expose dramatically the limits of the concept of equal freedom of expression for all.

So, can one have a quiet democracy: a political culture claiming to offer a say for everybody, but actually encouraging an all-round silence of the subjects? (Silence of the sheep rather than the lambs.) The history of the movement for the freedom to speak in Britain has been, as this book has shown, a long struggle against those who would enforce silence upon seditious tongues. The freedom to talk and be heard was never freely given, and was for long resisted by any means necessary. In many countries of the world today such resistance to free speech remains successful and tacitly supported by governments which claim to be democratic. From Saudi Arabia, where, as Said K Aburish has reported, uncounted numbers of the subjects are tortured under the most barbarous conditions

36. D Zilo, *Democracy and Complexity: A Realist Approach*, Cambridge, 1992, p168.

for the crime of refusing to keep their mouths shut and succumb to the unelected governance of the ruling family, to China, where, as Liu Binyan so movingly recorded in his book *Tell The World*, more than 3000 people were killed and 120 000 were imprisoned for their participation in the Tianenman Square public gathering of June 1989, the freedom to meet in public and speak without regulation is deemed criminal.[37] Both of these countries remain major trading partners of the West, free from any sanctions resulting from their contempt for the most elementary principles of free speech and democracy. The 'democratic West' has remained effectively silent as the silence of the majority is assured in such countries by methods as bad or worse than those once employed in Britain. Indeed, to speak of such silencing as if it were now only an exotic disorder confined to the politically unsophisticated would be to ignore the authoritarian arrogance of ministers and managers in Britain who have enforced conditions in several areas of employment where to criticise the service in which one works (be it the Post Office, British Rail or geriatric care) has become a sackable offence. The case of John Guy, an orthopaedic surgeon at Worcester Royal Infirmary, whose patient wrote to her MP, Nicholas Ridley, after being told by the former that the NHS could not provide her with a hip operation because of government cuts, is exemplary. Ridley, who was then Secretary of State for the Environment, wrote to Tony Newton, then Minister of Health, stating: 'I would be glad if you could investigate this and see that the necessary action is taken to silence Mr Guy.'[38]

The dream – half misty democratic utopianism and half technocratic dystopian – of 'teledemocracy' (as FC Arterton has described it, and Ted Becker so enthusiastically promoted it)[39] suggests a remarkably silent and atomised process of interactivity. US Vice-President Al Gore's bid in March 1991 for novelty as advocate of the Global Information Infrastructure rhetorically dismissed the position of the overwhelming majority of the earth's inhabitants (including the impoverished millions in both his own country and Britain) who lack the prospect of purchasing any access, and less still equal access, to the proposed new democratic sphere:

37. SK Aburish, *The Rise, Corruption and Coming Fall of the House of Saud*, London, 1994; Liu Binyan with Ruan Ming and Xu Gang, *Tell the World: What Happened in China and Why*, London, 1989.
38. Cited in T Wright, *Citizens and Subjects: An Essay on British Politics*, London, 1994, pp22-3. See also Eileen Furson's article on confidentiality clauses and whistle-blowing, 'Still Gagging on the Truth', *Guardian*, 20 November 1996.
39. FC Arterton, *Teledemocracy: Can Technology Protect Democracy?*, London, 1987; T Becker, 'Teledemocracy: Bringing Power Back to the People', *Futurist*, December 1981, pp6-9.

'This GII will circle the globe with information superhighways on which all people can travel. The GII will not only be a metaphor for a functioning democracy, it will in fact promote the functioning of democracy by greatly enhancing the participation of citizens in decision-making. I see a new Athenian Age of Democracy forged in the fora the GII will create.'[40]

Those without the means of purchasing computers, access to the net and their own personal or corporate web sites will presumably be as powerful in this brave new world as were the slaves in the 'Athenian Age of Democracy'. As Jay Kinney has pertinently observed:

'Cyberspace is full of armchair mavericks and eccentric ideologues. But whatever the gyrations of political difference and originality amongst them, the onrushing logic of the integration of the world economy and world politics into a single unified whole may overshadow those distinctions, just as the boundaries between nations are becoming anachronistic in the face of the "global marketplace".'[41]

The specific nature of this new disenfranchisement rests upon an important distinction between information and communication. Too frequently the freedom to be informed is confused with the freedom to communicate: the former is passive and the latter actively empowering. A better informed populace need not necessarily be one with any real increase in its power to talk back to the informers, or to one another. As Howard Besser has rightly observed: 'On the information superhighway most people will be relegated to the role of information consumer.'[42] To shift from informing people to enabling them to communicate radically alters and inevitably democratises the process of talk. In local terms this means that agendas for discussion may not be pre-set by political or economic elites, and that soapboxes, whether real or in cyberspace, must be available to all without the supervisory control of either states or markets. Globally, this must mean establishing as a necessary condition of democratic discourse the equal access to discussion of all social groups, however marginalised politically or weak economically.

40. Speech at the International Telecommunications Union, Buenos Aires, 21 March 1994.
41. J Kinney, 'Is There a New Political Paradigm Lurking in Cyberspace?', in Z Sardar and JR Ravetz (ed), *Cyberfutures: Culture and Politics on the Information Superhighway*, London, 1996, p145.
42. H Besser, 'From Internet to the Information Superhighway', in *Resisting the Virtual Life: The Culture and Politics of Information*, California, 1995, p62.

The push-button democracy envisaged by info-technocrats is weakened not only by the vast numbers technologically estranged from it, and by its confinement to informing people of what is rather than opening up communication to what might be, but also by its dialogic narrowness. Attempts to broaden the communicative and democratic scope of the Internet, such as the Minnesota E-Democracy Project and UK Citizens' On-Line Democracy,[43] stand or fall on the principle of the extent to which they permit genuinely unmediated discourse in which any proposition or first principle can be brought to the arena of public discussion by anyone with something to say. The claim that a forum for free speech is being established requires both open access (which does not exist within the Internet), and freedom for people to set their own agenda. Mill's requirement for discourse to entertain all views and not only orthodox opinion is effectively ignored in a situation where surfers on the Internet can pass by any dissenting outlook with much greater ease than can shoppers being handed leaflets or addressed from a platform. As in the case of Italian media deregulation, a thousand voices might be available to be heard, but far from them being presented upon a 'level playing field' of discussion, those voices supported by the greatest investment have the means to cast themselves as the dominant information locations, and discourage the search for alternative publicly-communicated truths.

Just as informing people is often confused with communication, so discussion is too often presented as being merely a feature of participation within existing structures of power. The notion that participation is inherently 'a good thing' for civil society is not valid. Participation in set-piece debates run by producers who are transparently contemptuous of those not setting the agenda can be tantamount to sustaining a political iniquity. This is the position taken by many pressure-group members who refuse to take part in badly-devised TV debates in which the impression of an exchange of ideas is crushed by production values that require the extreme compression of arguments, and, all too often, the sacrifice of open dialogue for entertaining ritual bear fights. There can be no doubt that participating in a 'discussion' which makes one a captive of someone else's agenda can diminish one's scope for autonomous expression. Fake discussions, just like the fake elections organised from time to time by dictatorial regimes, have nothing to do with democracy. A parallel delu-

43. Both of these projects are recent attempts to bring to citizens both political information and a forum for open discussions via the Internet. UK COD is based upon the relative success of the Minnesota project. I have acted as political consultant to the former.

sion is the frequent conflation of officially orchestrated 'consultation exercises' with meaningful participatory deliberation.

Revitalisation of the public sphere of democratic discussion should not be confused, as it often is, with simply generating more participation or facilitating more instantaneous forms of decision-making, however non-deliberative. The object of such revitalisation should be the creation of conditions of communication where political and other kinds of ideas, ideals and bodies of thought can be articulated and negotiated publicly, accessibly and meaningfully by anyone with a wish to influence society. This requires time for ideas to be developed through interactive discourse, free access to the most basic means of communicating ideas, and a refusal to place bounds upon the areas of expressible thoughts. Chomsky has argued that liberal capitalism encourages debate whilst maintaining tacit limits upon appropriate items for the agenda, so giving a false impression of free speech whilst actually maintaining the kind of thought control which he thinks is necessary to maintain the hegemony of market-supporting ideology:

'Debate cannot be stilled, and indeed, in a properly functioning system of propaganda, it should not be, because it has a system-reinforcing character if constrained within proper bounds. What is essential is to set the bounds firmly. Controversy may rage as long as it adheres to the presuppositions that define the consensus of elites, and it should be encouraged within these bounds, thus helping to establish these doctrines as the very condition of thinkable thought while reinforcing the belief that freedom reigns.'[44]

Until recently, public debate about the monarchy virtually excluded the republican option as being unworthy of entry into the arena of public opinion. Although such conservative exclusion has now been shattered by a combination of bold assaults upon this limit to the expressible by elements within the tabloid media and the self-destructiveness of certain prominent royal figures, the question remains of how the gates to the realm of acceptably expressible opinion are controlled. Even more is this the case with discussion about the role of the market. Traditionally, a role existed within public democratic discourse for non-market solutions to problems, including the proposition that market allocation of resources is obsolete and should be replaced by a better form of social organisation.

44. N Chomsky, *Necessary Illusions: Thought Control in Democratic Societies*, London, 1989, p48.

Regardless of the merits of such a position, and the credibility or otherwise of the current orthodoxy that a non-market solution was tried in certain countries and inevitably failed, it seems now that there is an increasing refusal to permit within the realm of publicly expressible opinions any ideas which deviate from the first principle of the market. Too often what passes for discussion fails to allow time for first principles to be contested, imposing an implicit censorship upon primary issues which inevitably diminishes the scope for democratically discussing subsequent ones. The debate about how to slaughter cattle proceeds with indifference to the vegetarian debate about whether to kill them at all; the debate about how to sell public services to consumers/customers ignores the question of whether services should be produced for sale at all. Public discussion of central assumptions is discouraged on the basis that the debate of secondary or peripheral questions is sufficient to constitute practical free speech. The setting of boundaries around expressible opinions becomes easier the more centralised the main locations of public discourse become. If these communications centres are controlled by people who are unelected and largely unaccountable to the public, as is the case with most of the existing mass media, this leaves the power of determining and defining the inexpressible dangerously beyond democratic culture, with tacit censorship of certain primary issues more a reflection of elitist consensus than anything resembling a conspiracy.

Recent developments in the analysis of public opinion, notably those arising from Elizabeth Noelle-Neumann's major work, *The Spiral of Silence: Public Opinion – Our Social Skin*, adds to our understanding of the unexpressed and the inexpressible aspects of public discussion. According to this radical revision of definition: 'Public opinions are attitudes or behaviours one must express in public if one is not to isolate oneself; in areas of controversy or change, public opinions are those attitudes one can express without running the danger of isolating oneself.'[45] A distinction is drawn between the manifest function of public opinion, according to which it is regarded as a rational function in the process of informing governments of the public will, and the latent function, which sees public opinion as an instrument for social control. Whoever determines public opinion may isolate, reject and ostracise those who refuse to go along with his outlook. According to this model of public opinion, the great fear of most people is the isolation and/or embarrassment which they

---

45. E Noelle-Neumann, *The Spiral of Silence: Public Opinion – Our Social Skin*, Chicago, 1993, p178.

will suffer if they deviate from public opinion; therefore they constantly try to find out what public opinion is, using quasi-statistical methods of discovery mainly dependent upon media information, and express or conceal their views depending upon the effects anticipated. This is not to say that people will never speak their own minds, but that generally speaking, and with varying intensity depending upon the number of strangers before whom they might be embarrassed, people who reject the basic principles of the majority tend to keep quiet about their dissent. Noelle-Neumann accepts that a hard core of vocal dissenters will always be in existence, but that the vast majority would rather conform to what they believe conventional wisdom to be, or remain silent about their doubts, rather than risk embarrassment or isolation. Supported by psychological tests conducted by Asch and Milgram, the impressive analyses of talk by Erving Goffman, and considerable opinion poll data from the Allensbach Centre in Germany, Noelle-Neumann offers an explanation for political silence which is highly convincing, and, though never explicitly connected, is in line with Chomsky's view about 'the limits of the expressible'. Interestingly, the early notions of public opinion as the result of considered public deliberation, such as that of Lowell in 1913 and Young in 1923, coincided with a period when open public discourse did have more of a real life within Western political culture.[46]

A good illustration of the latent function of public opinion was the climate surrounding the abolition of the Greater London Council (GLC). Opinion polls, in which Londoners could express their views in secrecy, showed that the vast majority of them supported the GLC and its radical policies. The chorus of disdain and abuse by the media, particularly the tabloid press, against the 'loony left' as epitomised by the GLC meant that publicly-expressed opinion tended to disown or remain silent about the GLC; only a hard core of left wing supporters constituted the main defence of the GLC, leaving the vast majority, including Neil Kinnock and the Labour shadow government, too embarrassed to declare openly their support for a privately supported but publicly ridiculed institution. When, in 1992, the public opinion polls were seen to be more wrong than ever in forecasting the general election result, one explanation for this rested upon the 'spiral of silence' theory: people refused to state publicly, or even to pollsters, their dissent from the perceived lead of the Labour Party over the Conservatives, but in the secrecy of the polling booth

46. AL Lowell, *Public Opinion and Popular Government*, New York, 1913; JT Young, *The New American Government and Its Work*, New York, 1923.

pursued what many of them had long held to be in their self-interest and voted Conservative.

The 'spiral of silence' theory points to an important correlation between people's dependence upon conventional wisdom, mainly provided by the mass media, and their fear of taking an independent stance. It follows from this that the less communication is dominated by centralised, controlling sources, and the more that public discourse comes to be integrated into autonomous areas of social culture, as was the case in the days of unregulated street-corner discussion, the easier it will be to break the spiral of silence. If, as the contemporary democratic theorists suggest, the most important aspect of democratic culture is free discussion, the conclusion must be that any conditions which intensify the 'spiral of silence' are bad for democracy, and any which allow people to communicate with a minimum of mediation are good for democracy.

Should we conclude from this that the mass media, as such, are bad for democracy? Is the only democratic way forward to be found in a romantic return to the street-corner meeting – or whatever its contemporary equivalent might be? The earliest critics of the media tended to present the problem in terms of this dichotomy. For example, speaking in a Guildhall lecture in the late 1960s on what was then the rather unexplored subject of 'The Politics of Television', Richard Crossman argued:

'Before television the place where the political activist traditionally went to understand the issues and make up his [sic] own mind, was the closed [sic] party meeting where he could hear the opponent cross-examined. In the television age it seems to me that the fairest way to present the politician to the viewer is in his natural element. Take the television cameras both into the closed meetings where politics are quietly discussed amongst friends and on to the hustings.'[47]

Failure of the TV companies to pursue this course, warned Crossman presciently, 'may well be responsible for making the next general election the first in which public discussion was rendered impossible'. For Crossman, the media could only be undisruptive to democratic culture if it merely reflected what was already going on, rather than attempting to construct its own theatre of artificial discourse. The early advice to the media offered by Stephen King-Hall regarded its putative role in creating a pluralistic public sphere:

47. R Crossman, *The Politics of Television: TV and the Political Party Image*, London, 1969, p35.

'The school broadcast talk brings the child in the rural school into direct relationship with Mr Baldwin defending democracy. It could – and if I had my way it would – bring that same child into a similar relationship with Mr Lansbury on socialism and Sir Oswald Mosley defending fascism, and Mr Pollitt or Mr Mann making the case for communism.'[48]

This points towards a possible use of the media to create something like a broadcast Speakers' Corner, but still a rather paternalistic one: the categories of thought and suitable speakers to represent them would still be determined by the media elite; the length of time to address the people would be limited, and the people's chance to talk back non-existent. More recent development in talk radio, despite the severe limitations already observed, might be seen as an extension of King-Hall's basically democratic intention of using the media to let every opinion be voiced. In his penetrating study *The Media and Democracy*, John Keane rehearses a libertarian alternative to all forms of state-regulated communication; such 'dispersed networks of communication', he suggests, 'indicate ways in which, especially among the less powerful citizenry, new forms of "solidarity among the shaken" (Patocka) can be developed against the atomising effects of modern life. Communicative networks can help to offset the tendency of the mass media to pile discontinuity onto us, to wash away memories, to dissolve and fast-cut, to throw away yesterday's papers.' Building up the case for such non-state-regulated 'bush networks', Keane argues with convincing force:

'They enable citizens to squeeze the slave out of themselves, drop by drop. They help them to cultivate the virtues of democratic citizenship: prudence, judgement, eloquence, resourcefulness, courage, self-reliance, sensitivity to power, common sense. Communications networks renew the old insight that the decentralisation of power is sometimes the most effective cure for an undue parochialism; that through involvement in local organisations, citizens overcome their localism.'[49]

Keane ultimately rejects the libertarian option, but less persuasively than he has outlined it. There is much to be said for the argument that the real deregulation of the media (not to be confused with commercial deregulation, which has amounted to little more than the flogging of the airwaves to state-approved investors) could indeed create the

48. Cited in M Pegg, *Broadcasting and Society, 1918-1939*, London, 1983, p190.
49. J Keane, *The Media and Democracy*, Cambridge, 1991, pp145-6.

condition for a synthesis between the technology of mass communication and the needs for interactive, deliberative, untrammelled discourse within a thinking, speaking and listening public sphere. Arguably, the move away from the mass media as the guardian of the inexpressible, serving to perpetuate the 'spiral of silence' to the point where democracy exists in name only, and towards a media which facilitates unregulated public discussion, is the most crucial political issue of our age. Nicholas Garnham argues:

'It is a commonplace to assert that public communication lies at the heart of the democratic process; that citizens require, if their equal access to the vote is to have any substantive meaning, equal access also to sources of information and equal opportunities to participate in the debates from which political decisions rightly flow. I want to argue that it follows that changes in media structure and media policy, whether these stem from economic developments or from public intervention, are properly political questions of as much importance as the question of whether or not to introduce proportional representation, of relations between local and national government, of subsidies to political parties; that the policies of Western European governments towards cable TV and satellite broadcasting is as important as the attitude towards the development of a United Europe; that the FCC's policy towards broadcast regulation is as important as that of the states' rights and that politicians, political scientists and citizens concerned with the health and future of democracy neglect these issues at their peril.'[50]

Yet the conspicuous absence of any substantial policies by the major parties to address the undemocratic culture of the existing channels of mass communication suggests that they benefit too much from the existing arrangements to seek to change them, as collusion by both the main British political parties with the Murdoch Empire indicates – not least in relation to the cross-party silence over Murdoch's efforts to monopolise the benefits of digital TV. Where once power elites severed the tongues of dissenters, perhaps now the policy is to switch off the microphone; a more civilised, but no less undemocratic, form of gagging. If the modern resistance to unregulated discussion, in Britain if not elsewhere, draws the line well short of massacring workers in Manchester or surrounding the Hyde Park gates with police, we have yet to see what response there would

50. N Garnham, *Capitalism and Communication: Global Culture and the Economics of Information*, London, 1994, p104.

be to a struggle for equal access to and control of the contemporary means of mass communication.

Meanwhile, the metaphorical invocation of Speakers' Corner as the imagined forum for the freeborn Englishman to speak his mind remains a popular cultural reference in the description of British democracy. Nicholas Jones, in observing the important historical transformation from the days when TV cameras followed politicians to our own times when politicians run to where the cameras are to be found, writes about College Green to which MPs are to be seen:

'... trooping out of the Commons chamber in ever greater numbers. On busy days four or five television crews, plus reporters and producers, could be seen at work; at times of high political drama there might be double that number. Judging by the fascination of passers-by, who started to cluster round to listen to MPs being questioned, the parliamentary dialogue on College Green began to emerge as a weekday alternative to the soap-box oratory of Speakers' Corner in Hyde Park.'[51]

The allusion deceives. The culture of Speakers' Corner rejects soundbites, and crowds rarely leave posturing unpunctured or evasion unexposed. At Speakers' Corner anyone could take the platform, even though none is ever guaranteed an audience. College Green's attraction is that those speaking are not 'anyone', but the 'somebodies' recognisable from TV, feeding into an incestuous circuit of predictable talk leading to greater recognition leading to greater opportunities still to churn out the clichés before the cameras in what is far from being, by any reasonable description, a democratic 'dialogue'. It would be better to present College Green as the antithesis of an environment characterised by free and open dialogue. It is important for these two models of democratic communication to be differentiated. Speaking in recent times to groups of parliamentarians and political activists from the 'new democracies' of Central and Eastern Europe, one has been at pains to counter their own frequent interpretations of democratic dialogue as comprising the right of political factions to speak at length, and then make way for rival factions to state their case as if the other has not spoken. Dialogue, one has suggested to such audiences, entails hearing as well as speaking and interactive, interrogative discussion as much as, if not more than, simply speechifying.

John Keane offers his readers a vision of Speakers' Corner as a demo-

51. N Jones, *Soundbites and Spin Doctors: How Politicians Manipulate the Media – And Vice Versa*, London, 1995, p16.

cratic utopia, with 'legal and financial encouragement' provided so as 'to guarantee rights of access during certain hours on radio and television to individuals, groups and programme makers'. This 'would help to build the electronic equivalent of Speakers' Corner and add a much-needed new element of spontaneous drama, fun and intellectual vitality to the media'.[52]

In his bid to contrive such fun and vitality as Conservative leader, John Major, a man hardly renowned for these characteristics, has utilised the imagery of the open-air meeting during the course of his election campaigning. In an early party political broadcast of the successful 1992 campaign, entitled *John Major: The Journey*, viewers were told how the teenage Major, a passionate Tory even then, had spoken on his soapbox at Brixton market. Had he actually ever done so? If so, why had he learned so little from this experience about the skills of oratory? And, if the story is not apocryphal, will he have been the last Prime Minister to learn the art of political speech-making within such a totally unmediated setting? During the 1992 campaign, Major visited Bolton, and, after being barracked by left wing newspaper sellers, stood up on a Conservative Central Office packing case (subsequently referred to by journalists as a soapbox) and put his case. It was a novel and successful gesture, and led to more stunts of this kind, the later ones being better stage-managed. The obsessive fascination with this street corner stunt points to a recognition that somewhere beneath the theatrical gesture lay a genuine nostalgia for an unmediated form of communication. Shaun Woodward, the Conservative election strategist, observed that 'his use of the soapbox was further evidence of the figure he had always presented himself to be'; for Lord Wakeham, it took the 'broadcast image of John Major on his soapbox to capitalise on his popular personality'. Max Atkinson, in his droll account of 'Majorspeak', noted that 'making a virtue out of ordinariness' was 'apparent in the Prime Minister's decision to campaign on the streets from a traditional soapbox'. *The Sun*, almost orgasmic in its nostalgic joy at the sight of the plain bloke on his soapbox, 'highlighted the populist connotations of Major's [hustings soapbox] tactic, while avoiding the risk of taking it too seriously', by stating that 'John Major revived a crate tradition', and then running a half-page photo-feature entitled 'How To Build Your Own Major Soapbox'.[53] In his pre-election conference speech in 1996, Major concluded by informing the Tory faithful that they would

52. Keane, op cit, p156.
53. I Crewe and B Gosschalk (eds), *Political Communications: The General Election of 1992*, Cambridge, 1995, pp7, 35, 139-40, 259.

always be able to spot him during the coming election campaign because he would be the chap standing in the middle of the crowd arguing his case. The soapbox imagery was clearly intended to suggest a return to old-fashioned channels of simple communication, in contrast to New Labour's impressively state-of-the-art media machine. The suggestion would have been rather less mendacious had it not been the case that the Conservative Party's own marketing machine was at that very moment being primed to ensure that the coming election campaign would be largely stage-managed and non-interactive, with Major's soapbox used as little more than a prop in his Norman Wisdomesque bid to play the common man with a message to impart. Even the usually loyal *Daily Mail* was prompted to wonder on 30 October 1996 how it was that if Major had learnt his oratory on the open-air platform, he was such a rotten communicator. The assumption that soapbox orators should be expected to be better at communicating. The real irony of Major's fabricated soapbox spontaneity was its utilisation of a communication strategy traditionally resorted to by those lacking access to the centre stage and the cameras, now being simulated from centre stage for the very benefit of the cameras. It marked a key moment in the drift from designer policies to designer discussion.

As political publicists parody the open-air meeting as a cheap and romantically evocative marketing image, transforming democratic tradition into camera-ready performance art, Speakers' Corner in the last years of the twentieth century stands as a rather pathetic parody of itself. In 1995 a competition organised by the Department of National Heritage sought proposals for the redesign of Speakers' Corner. The design improvement which was never considered would involve finding some speakers worthy of the site. Speakers' Corner has become an embarrassment, offering to the casual passer-by a freak-show of fanaticism and facile exhibitionism. It stands now as a monument to the self-fulfilling prophecy of those who believed that the man in the street was best left to his own brooding silence, for given a platform he will only make a fool of himself and waste the time of those listening to him. It was not always so: the Corner had always attracted its share of religious zealots, cranks and those in search of a free licence to abuse an audience with impunity, but they were never in the majority. Both the police and veteran orators, such as Lord Soper speaking from his wheelchair in the late 1990s, declare their exasperation at the behaviour of gangs of offensive, fascistic, organised disrupters whose sole objective is not to discuss or even to heckle, but to break up meetings. Their ugly presence, serving as the unwitting gravediggers of an atrophying institution, owes much to the long decline of verbal political literacy as well as the growth of a raucous, ruthless insensitivity in styles of public entertainment. An unnerving return to the dark age of the cockfight characterises much that happens at Speakers' Corner these days. Equally indicative of this return to the dark ages is the domination of the Corner by rival Christian and Muslim fundamentalists. As Milly Jenkins observed in the *Independent on Sunday* in May 1996: 'The country's most famous bastion of free speech and lawful free assembly has become the home of fundamentalists who are prepared to use violence to silence their opponents.' All of this contrasts starkly with the condition of the place only a few decades ago, within the memory of most people who believe that democratic discussion is a civilising process. Clearly, it is symptomatic of something more terminally significant than the institution itself that Speakers' Corner as a place to which men like my father could take their children to see real democratic discussion in action is unlikely to be available for the next generation to witness. It is not the place itself, but the political culture within which it awkwardly sits as an emblem of a lost tradition, which has taken a turn for the worse. Britain has become one big non-speakers', non-listeners' corner. Tongues once cut out are now poked out at authority — a gesture of both despair and impotence.

Index